W9-BFS-852

The Quick and Easy Guide to
Project Management

*Keeping your projects on track,
on time and on budget*

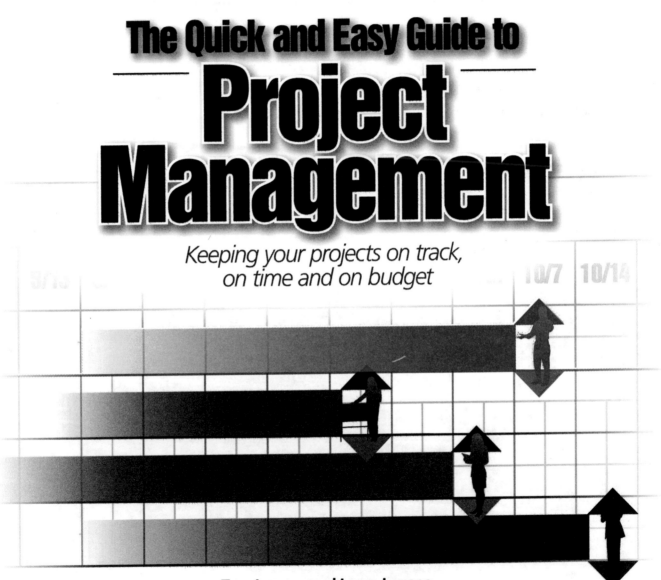

Tom Lagana and Laura Lagana

SkillPath® Publications

Editor: Bill Cowles

Cover design: Jason Sprenger

Layout: Barbara Hartzler

ISBN: 978-1-934589-28-1

Printed in the United States of America

The Quick and Easy Guide to
Project
Management

*Keeping your projects on track,
on time and on budget*

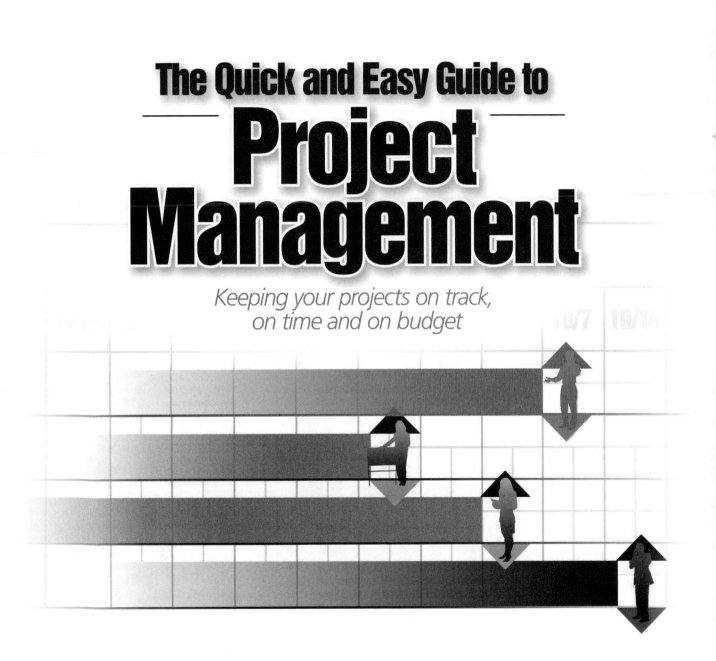

With love and appreciation, we dedicate this book to God, and to everyone, past, present and future, who improves our world by sharing their skills and talents through projects.

Table of Contents

Introduction

What would the world be like without successful project management? From unfinished roads, inferior bridges and partial buildings to abandoned inventions and discoveries left undiscovered, our existence would be exceedingly different from what we sometimes take for granted.

By virtue of human nature, people tend to look for simple solutions to problems. The same holds true for people seeking a method of moving their projects forward or getting them "unstuck." Consequently, this book is presented in a format such that anyone can pick it up, open to a page and find sound advice and suggestions they can apply instantly. A summary of helpful hints and "how-to" exercises appears at the conclusion of each chapter to enhance the learning process.

The Quick and Easy Guide to Project Management is designed for people who are doing the actual work on projects at their workplace, in their personal lives and in their communities. Not everyone we encounter in project management seminars has the title of Project Manager, nor do they consider themselves as such. They are, however, the people who are responsible for getting projects done, in addition to dealing with their other responsibilities and who do not necessarily have people reporting to them. Ultimately, they tend to feel they are carrying out projects on their own without realizing they can achieve success by enlisting the help of others.

Most project managers realize that not everyone they supervise is ready to take the plunge into complex project management techniques. Project managers also understand the importance of knowing the basic concepts, even when using more advanced techniques. Even so, common sense is not always common practice, and we all need reminders.

Why Are You Reading This Book?

This is a good question to ask yourself any time you are about to invest valuable time in an endeavor. What benefits do you foresee? What are your objectives? What would you like to have happen as a result?

List the skills you want to improve and sharpen when working on projects:

_____

_____

_____

_____

Bring Project Awareness to the Foreground

The more you are conscious of how project management affects your daily life, the more likely you are to make it a natural part of your being.

In the next 24 hours, notice the projects that are either in progress or recently completed and list them below:

_____

_____

_____

_____

Quick Tips on Developing Your Skills

- Before beginning a new project, step back and evaluate the tools you will use

- Practice, continue to develop and sharpen project management skills by volunteering for community projects. It's a win-win situation.

- No matter how much or how little experience you think you have, everyone has something to bring to the table. Your perspective is important and valuable.

- Become aware of the skills you want to sharpen when working on projects

- Notice what projects are currently underway within your community, in addition to those in your workplace

Reprinted by permission of Matt Matteo

Chapter 1:

Evaluate Where You Are

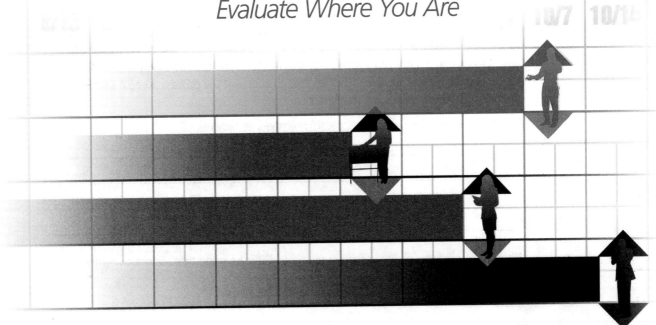

As you begin any project, you have an opportunity to start fresh, take a step back and evaluate where you are and where you want to go. What tools, skills and talents do you already have in your tool bag? Which ones need to be sharpened and polished? Is something no longer effective that should be removed? What could be added? Are time-wasting activities bogging your down? Do you need to become more organized?

Tailor Your Tools to Your Project

Keep it simple and streamlined (KISS). Not every organizational tool is needed for every project. Although it's beneficial to be familiar with all the tools available, just because one exists doesn't mean you have to use it. Tailor your tools to suit your project. A good rule of thumb is: When your projects are going well (i.e., you are meeting deadlines and staying within budget and the final product looks like it's supposed to), then keep up the excellent work. Things that are not progressing well should signal the need to evaluate exactly what is happening and consider other options to augment the process. Keep it simple and streamlined as much as possible and practical.

What tools are you and your project team members already using?

_____

_____

_____

_____

What tools could you and your project team members be using that are not currently being utilized?

_____

_____

_____

_____

Balancing Other Things

Besides the projects you are currently working on, consider your other work—those day-to-day tasks and responsibilities. Remember the projects and goals in your personal life. Be sure to relate the concepts and techniques of managing projects to all aspects of your life (e.g., moving, vacation, luncheon event, professional certification, career change, weight loss, fundraiser, party and business trip). The tools you use on projects at work are beneficial and can be applied to your own personal projects as well. Make them part of everyday living and allow them to become second nature. You are already using them, so just bring them to the center of your consciousness and put them to work.

Think of a project as if it were a computer system, with two parts working together in perfect harmony—the hardware and the software. Consider as the hardware the nuts and bolts or organizational tools and, as the software, the soft skills you employ to get yourself and others motivated to do what it takes to complete a successful project.

Recognize When You Have a Project and When You Don't

What constitutes a project? Often people refer to some of the work they do as a project when it isn't. Tasks that need to be performed on a continuous or recurring basis are not considered to be projects. For example, if you create a new form to use at work, the creation of the new form is a project. Using the form after its creation is a process. Many concepts you use for projects can also be used for your other work or processes, but it's advantageous to recognize which ones are projects and which are not. To help you decide, ask the following questions:

- Does it have a start date?

- Does it have a completion date?

- Are there steps that need to be finished in a specific order?

- Is its success dependent on other people?

- Is there an end result that will create something new or different than when you started?

What if you were planning a trip? Commuting to work each day, since it recurs regularly with the same outcome, is a process rather than a project. If you were planning a trip to Europe, whether for business or pleasure, you could regard it as a project. Your trip has a start date and time, an end date and time, it is dependent on other people to be successful and the end result or outcome will be your memories, souvenirs and photographs of a superb European vacation.

List the projects you are currently working on in your workplace:

_____

_____

_____

_____

List the projects you are currently working on in your personal life:

_____

_____

_____

_____

Once you have listed your projects, prioritize them. Is one more important than the others? An easy way to decide is to choose two projects and ask yourself, "If I have to make a choice between these two and I only have enough time to do one of them, which one will it be?" When prioritizing your projects, for each one ask yourself, "What are the benefits for my organization, my project team and me?" List those benefits next to each project name. Although you prioritize your projects, you may find that you still need to work on some of them every day so they can all move forward.

As deadlines approach, notice if any top priorities need to be adjusted. Following is an example of several projects with their assigned priorities and sequence. (*Note:* Some personal projects are integrated with business projects in cases where one influences the other.)

1. Write new procedure

2. Business trip to Indiana

3. File taxes

4. Estimate cost of upgrading system

5. Vacation in Hawaii

6. Finish Bill's report

7. Integrate new business in existing financial software

8. Get new computer

9. Learn Microsoft® Project

10. Move office to another building

11. Family get-together in Maine

Assign the number "1" to the project that has the highest priority based on its importance and urgency. Then assign the number "2" and so on until each project has a number. Although there are more scientific ways to calculate a priority number, your gut feeling is usually the best indicator. Even with more sophisticated methods, you can easily fudge the calculations based on your intuition; therefore, avoid the extra work unless someone asks to see your reasoning.

At this point, you may be thinking: "But I have to do *all* the projects. That's what my boss expects." Always remember that your boss, your clients and countless other people you work for and with can provide you with endless projects, potentially creating impossible situations. Listing the projects gives you an overview of your existing workload, helps you to put it into perspective and, most importantly, gives you something tangible to discuss with your boss and others. When you know there is more on your plate than you can realistically complete successfully, it's time to negotiate, reprioritize and possibly ask that some of your projects be reassigned to others. Empower yourself to ask for help when help is needed.

List the projects you foresee at work, then prioritize them:

_____

_____

_____

_____

List the projects you foresee in your personal life, then prioritize them:

_____

_____

_____

_____

Some people can work on numerous projects simultaneously and still manage to get most of them completed, while others may work on various projects and never seem to complete even one. If you fall into the latter category, it's essential to prioritize your projects and then focus.

Keeping yourself motivated is also important. Completing a project is fulfilling and encourages you to move forward to complete other projects, or at least to get them fired up and moving in the right direction.

Whenever a new project enters the picture, ask yourself and your project team members, "Where does this fit in?" Re-evaluate your list and reprioritize as needed. Communicate with the right people to ensure that your top priorities are aligned with those of your boss, your department and your organization. You could be working on what you think is a priority project, only to find out that it's not important or urgent to the people you need to please in order to be successful.

> Not only do you need to do your project right, you also need to do the right projects.

What Is Already Working Well? What Needs Improvement?

Make a list of those things you and your team members are doing on your projects and within your department that are working well. If you are working with a project team, first ask each person to make their list independently, then assemble your group and compare lists. Create a combined list that incorporates the ideas of everyone. Some people may want to turn the question around and list what is not working. If this occurs, avoid criticism and actively listen to the feedback. Pay attention to cues you can use to turn the dialogue around toward a more positive vein.

Create a second list: "Areas That Need Improvement." Notice the varying perspectives. Several members of your group may indicate that the team communicates effectively, while others may feel that this is an area that warrants improvement. Everyone is entitled to their own perspective. Awareness is the first step toward making changes for the better.

List what is working well on your projects and in your department:

_____

_____

_____

_____

List the areas that need improvement:

_____

_____

_____

_____

Next to each area that requires improvement, answer the question "What can we do to make this better?" Include at least two options to solve the problem. Look for specific action items and consider who can take action.

Know the Lingo

Every organization and field of work has its own terms, jargon and acronyms. Because they fear being perceived as inexperienced, people sometimes are reluctant to ask for "lingo" clarification. Even the most knowledgeable people, working in a different company or on a unique type of project, may find themselves unfamiliar with some of the terms people are using. It is always advantageous to inquire. Don't assume that everyone but you knows the jargon.

And when you're the one using the jargon, a rule of thumb is: The first time you write an acronym or use special jargon, define it. Similarly, when speaking with others, ensure they understand the terms you're using without talking down to them. The main purpose of communication is to express, not to impress. Using terms correctly allows people to have confidence in you and gives them an added sense of self-reliance as well. When everyone speaks the same language it is easier to build rapport.

In future chapters we will discuss various terms associated with projects, including: critical path, Network Diagram, slack time, float time, WBS, crash, dependencies, Gantt Charts, PERT, CPM, paralleling of tasks and scope creep. If any of these terms are new to you, they will become clear as we proceed and explain the concepts and terms in future chapters.

Common Sense Isn't Always Common Practice

Every day, we exercise the power of free will and succumb to human nature innumerable times. For instance, just because we may know that something is good for us doesn't guarantee we will do it (e.g., exercising regularly or fastening our seat belt). Common sense isn't always common practice. Once you and your team clearly identify what is working well and what needs to improve, a support system develops, creating a more positive working environment. Hence, a keen sense of what should be common practice for the success of the project begins to evolve.

Have you ever started working on a project without being quite sure what you were doing? If you're like most people, this happens more often than you might imagine. You're expected to plow forward without direction, which often leads to having to start the project over again.

Before you and your team get too far into a project, it's best to evaluate what you know about it and how you feel about working on it. Unfortunately, most people aren't willing to share that information with those who need to know—and if you're the one responsible for the project's success, that person could be YOU.

Inside every large project is a small project trying to get out.

Imagine your car is in the shop. What if the mechanics working on it weren't quite sure what they were doing, didn't have the right skills or weren't using the proper tools to fix it? You are the one paying for parts and labor. This inefficiency will cost you dearly. The same is true with your projects. Whether you are responsible for the entire project or simply a portion of it, it is prudent to get off on the right foot by asking everyone associated with it to complete an anonymous written survey. This gives people the freedom to share what they truly think and how they really feel, so you can take corrective action before everyone makes further progress toward implementing the project.

The following survey has been given to hundreds of people working on projects. If you look at the first question as an example, the average score is only slightly higher than 7 (on a scale of 1 to 10, with 10 being the highest). How would you feel if you were responsible for the success of a project and the people working on it didn't have a clear idea of what their project was supposed to accomplish?

Project Management Survey

How would you rate the following areas in your organization? Circle one number for each statement.

Poor				Average					Excellent

We have a clear idea of what our projects are supposed to accomplish.

1	2	3	4	5	6	7	8	9	10

We can describe specifically the limits of our resources.

1	2	3	4	5	6	7	8	9	10

Our projects are segmented into manageable pieces.

1	2	3	4	5	6	7	8	9	10

Our projects have written schedules.

1	2	3	4	5	6	7	8	9	10

Our projects consider the perspectives of all stakeholders.

1	2	3	4	5	6	7	8	9	10

Each project team member is committed to the project's successful completion.

1	2	3	4	5	6	7	8	9	10

Our project team members build effective agreements and think win-win.

1	2	3	4	5	6	7	8	9	10

Our project team willingly follows requests of others.

1	2	3	4	5	6	7	8	9	10

Our project team is motivated to be creative and imaginative.

1	2	3	4	5	6	7	8	9	10

What prevents you from getting your projects done on-time, within budget and to specification/quality?

_____

_____

What suggestions do you have to improve your organization's project management?

_____

_____

What is working well? _____

_____

> A project grows a year late one day at a time.

Know Thyself

All too often, people are "serving time" on their projects. This is unfair to the organization and other project team members, and especially, if you're the one doing it, to yourself. Before you go any further into defining and planning your project, ask yourself a few personal questions. If you don't want others to see your answers, don't write them down, but be truthful with yourself:

- Why are you working on this project?
- Do you enjoy working on the types of projects you are assigned?
- Should you quit this project?
- Would you rather work on other projects?
- Should you ask to work on a different project?
- Are you passionate about your work?
- Is your work in alignment with your personal goals and dreams?
- Should you change jobs or careers?

Quick Tips on Evaluating Where You Are

- Keep things as simple as possible
- Write down your work projects and post where you and others can see them
- List your personal projects and goals, posting them where you can see them
- Practice the basic principles of project management in all aspects of your life
- Be aware of what a project is and what it isn't
- Be aware of what your project is and what it isn't
- Write down the areas in which you want improvement to become evident
- Use acronyms and jargon appropriately
- Ask to work on projects that have meaning for you
- Identify time wasters and interruptions, then create an action plan to eliminate them

Furious activity does not necessarily equate to progress
and is no substitute for understanding.

Chapter 2:

Know What Success Means—
Define Your Project Goals

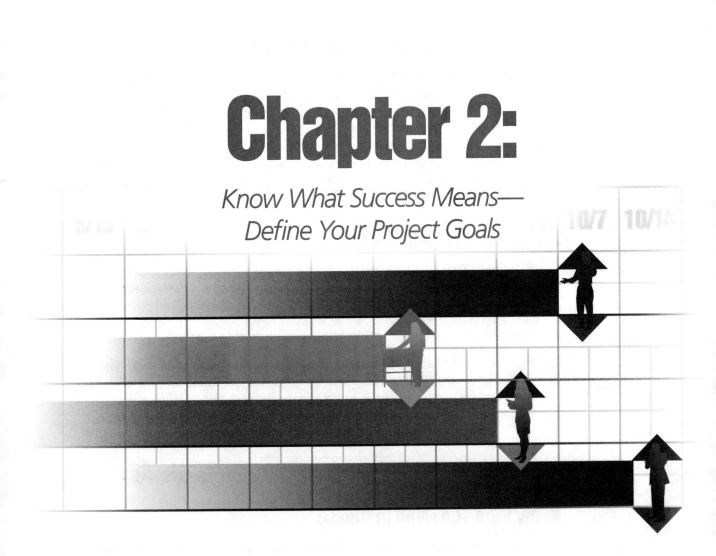

Why Are You Working on This Project?

Once you are assigned a project, it's important to first comprehend why the project is necessary. If you don't know, ask. Projects come about because of problems, needs or opportunities which develop into a strategy or plan. Knowing how the project fits into your organization's operations and why it needs to be done helps you and others working on the project to feel grounded. It brings more meaning and purpose to your project. Without a meaningful purpose it simply becomes more work. Knowing the purpose, finding meaning and aligning the project with your personal goals creates a win-win-win for your project, your organization and you.

Define Success and Scope

Before you begin your project, be aware of what it will take to be completed successfully. Although everyone knows this is advisable, it doesn't always become common practice. People don't set out to intentionally wreck a project, but if they fail to define, upfront, the expected end result, including all allowable variances, the outcome will be less than desirable.

Identify what the essentials are for your project to be successful. These are the must-haves. Without them, your project will be unsatisfactory. Along with the must-haves, identify what your non-essentials are. Non-essentials encompass the desirable, but not imperative, things that will enhance the project's success. In other words, they are nice to have but not vital.

There are times when the project team thinks that they are doing what the client expects and the client believes all is well, but the end product is unacceptable. For this reason, be certain to establish the goals of the project and begin with the end results in mind.

Know Who You Need to Please

To have a successful project involves identifying who you need to please in the end—your client. Periodically, project managers may realize that who they originally thought was their client turns out to be a different client at the end. There is also the possibility that the same project could have more than one client with conflicting goals.

For example, one client may control the cost, another may consider time to be a priority and a third may only be concerned about quality. Clients may be internal to your organization as well as external. In the Definition phase, identify all the key players you will need to please and recognize areas of conflict so you can address them near the beginning of your project. As you discover potential misalignments of project goals and objectives, move that information upward to higher management to settle. Then make certain the agreements are in writing, resembling a contract, to ensure everyone is headed in the right direction.

Define the End Result

Start by defining what your end result will be. In project management terms, these are known as "deliverables." Examples of 12 deliverables are:

1. Write new procedure
2. Test equipment
3. Evaluate new software application
4. Install new phone system
5. Upgrade server
6. Integrate financial systems
7. Train all employees
8. Produce new product
9. Construct new facility
10. Upgrade kitchen
11. Build new home
12. Write a users' manual

List typical deliverables for your projects at work and/or in your personal life:

_____

_____

_____

_____

Although you may know what your deliverables will look like when they're done, others may not have enough information. The examples above are somewhat vague unless you define each deliverable more clearly.

Seek a Reality Check

Find someone from outside your project who is unfamiliar with it and willing to assist you in this next exercise. Explain your project deliverables to them. Friends and family members can help you determine just how clearly you communicate what you want to accomplish.

For each of the 12 examples of typical deliverables just listed, invite your assistant to ask you the following corresponding questions:

1. **Write new procedure:** What must the new procedure describe?

2. **Test equipment:** Why is the equipment being tested?

3. **Evaluate new software application:** What will the new software application do?

4. **Install new phone system:** How many phones? For whom? What will the new phone system do that the old one didn't?

5. **Upgrade server:** Upgrade the server to what? Is it faster? If so, how fast?

6. **Integrate financial systems:** Which financial systems need to be integrated?

7. **Train all employees:** Who exactly needs to be trained and why? What does the training need to include?

8. **Produce new product:** What are the specifications of the new product?

9. **Construct new facility:** What will the new facility produce? What is the capacity?

10. **Upgrade kitchen:** What are the dimensions of the kitchen? What equipment will be added or upgraded?

11. **Build new home:** How big is the new home? How many bedrooms does it have? How many bathrooms? Does it have a garage? Is it attached? What about a basement?

12. **Write a users' manual:** Who are the users and what needs to be in the manual?

Make sure you do not divulge sensitive and confidential information about your project to anyone on the outside.

Visualize Success

Can you visualize your project upon its successful completion? Based on what you have defined so far, picture your end result. How clearly can you see it? Do you see people using what you created? Do they have smiles on their faces, happily using your deliverable? As you continue to define the success of your project, be sure to include enough information so that you can measure it.

Place the Specifics in Writing

In addition to visualizing the success of your end product, it's important to write down specifically what spells success for this project. When you put pen to paper (or keystrokes to a screen) and write down what you want, you are sending a signal to your brain and subconscious that your intentions are resolute. The more information you feed your subconscious, the more likely it will assist you in discerning things that will help you reach your goal.

Know the Time, Cost and Performance— the Triple Constraints

The success of your project is based on more than simply producing an output or deliverable that is within specification. In addition, it means getting your project done on time and within budget. In this early stage of defining project parameters or dimensions, it's important to establish your goals and objectives by recording everything you know about the Time, Cost and Performance aspects of your project. These are also known as the **Triple Constraints**.

This definition is a high-level overview of what success means in relation to Time, Cost and Performance. It is not intended to convey specific details of every task and activity, which will happen later in the Planning stage. First, define "The What" (What needs to be done?). "The How" is the plan. Before moving forward, define the criteria for Time, Cost and Performance:

- **Time** refers to your start date, finish date, duration of tasks and other time-sensitive milestones or deadlines that occur during your project: increments of time that you are able to identify specifically in order to complete your project. In this case, time does not refer to time savings expected as a result of completing your project.

- **Cost**, also known as Budget, refers to how much the project will cost in terms of materials, supplies and cost of the people working on your project. Cost in this case does not refer to any cost savings expected as a result of completing your project.

- **Performance**, also referred to as Quality, Quality Standard, Scope, Output or Specification, refers to the characteristics and standards of your deliverable as well as time savings and cost savings expected as a result of your project.

Once you have identified specific key words to define your project in terms of Time, Cost and Performance, document these so you and others can see them in writing. Write a sentence or two to define each of the Triple Constraints. Make your project goals as clear and concise as possible. A fuzzy goal produces fuzzy results and is the main reason why some projects fizzle out.

At this juncture, ask yourself: "Does this project make sense?" In addition, explain your project to others who are associated with it. Include at least one person who is unfamiliar with it. Ask them to paraphrase aloud their interpretation of your definition of success. Observe their nonverbals. Are you certain they really understand what you want to do? If there is an inkling of doubt, it indicates you may need to clarify your definition of success.

A SMART Test for Defining Success

A tried-and-true method for goal setting, the acronym SMART helps smooth the process of defining the success of project goals.

The *"S"* stands for:

- **Specific:** Make your definitions of Time, Cost and Performance precise enough that you can visualize them in detail. Be sure that your goals are specific enough so that others can also understand them.

The *"S"* in SMART may have additional meanings, including:

- **Scripted:** Ensure that your definition of success is written down, making an imprint on your subconscious.

- **Self-talk:** What are you saying to yourself about your project? Do you truly believe it's possible? What are others who are working on your project saying to themselves? Is their self-talk positive?

The *"M"* in SMART stands for:

- **Measurable:** There is an old saying: "If you can't measure it, you can't get it." When defining success, know what you want so explicitly that you can measure it. Putting the specifications of your deliverable in writing allows you and others to adequately measure whether you actually achieve the project goals or not.

The *"M"* in SMART may also stand for:

- **Meaningful:** The more meaningful the project is to you and your project team, the more likely it is that everyone will be motivated to do their best. So what exactly are the benefits to you and others upon completion of this project? Ask yourself: "Why am I working on this project?" Continue asking that question and write down your responses until your list includes at least two that help others. Suppose you are working on a project to write a new procedure or upgrade a computer system. What else are you accomplishing in the process? The end result could also be to help create a brighter and happier future for you and others. Through this project, are you protecting the lives of others, enhancing society or helping our planet? The more meaning you find in doing ordinary work and projects, the more you will continue to motivate yourself.

The **"A"** in SMART stands for:

- **Agreed-upon:** Most times, you need the agreement of others in order to get your project done successfully. At work, you may not be empowered to independently select a project on which to work. Most likely it will require approval from others. First, determine whom you need to please. You also will need the agreement of others you will rely on for the successful completion of your project, including your project team and support staff.

The **"A"** in SMART may have additional meanings, including:

- **Activated:** Action is the key to getting anything done; otherwise, it's just a wish, a hope, a plan or a dream. You may have the most brilliant plan in the world, but unless it's activated or carried out, it will never come to pass.

- **Aligned:** Goals should be in alignment with your values and vision. As with Agreed-upon, your project goals need to be aligned with the requirements of your department, company and upper management. And when it comes to setting *personal* goals, you will want to be in alignment with the important people in your life.

The **"R"** in SMART stands for:

- **Realistic:** Have you ever worked on a project with an impossible deadline or budget and you were behind schedule before you even started? For a project to be successful, make it realistic and build in contingencies. In cases where upper management, clients and customers are asking for something unrealistic, do your homework and enlighten them as to why you need more time or additional money to produce your deliverable to the desired specification. Your responsibility is to alert upper management and others when "The Impossible Project" is in the works.

The **"R"** in SMART may have additional meanings, including:

- **Review and Revise Regularly:** As time progresses on your project, other factors also will change. Make revisions along the way or you may find yourself being squeezed in the middle, unable to meet the demands of Time, Cost and Performance.

- **Reach:** Although you know what it takes for a project to be considered modestly successful, it is beneficial to identify what else is possible and desirable to strive for and achieve if additional time and money become available. Stretch and strive for the ideal. Reach for the nonessentials realistically.

The **"T"** in SMART stands for:

- **Time-framed:** What is your start date? When will you finish? What milestones need to be completed during the project? In your personal projects, set a realistic time frame to avoid the natural temptation to procrastinate. Vague terms like "as soon as possible" could imply "someday." Be precise and realistic when defining the time elements and estimates.

The **"T"** in SMART may have additional meanings, including:

- **Term (Short-term and Long-term):** Take into account not only the end of the project but also the short-term goals or milestones leading up to its completion. This gives everyone the feeling of closure and fulfillment; as you complete one step, you are motivated by the realization that you are moving forward productively.

- **Tell:** Communicate your project goals to everyone working on your project. Tell those you trust about your personal projects and goals. The act of telling others keeps you accountable and allows others to offer ideas that might help you in achieving your goals.

No Time Frame = No Urgency = Low Productivity

Know What You Want and Why

Once you know what you want and why you want it, you and those working alongside you on the project will be empowered to figure out how to make it happen. All it takes is paying the price in time and money.

Be the model of goal setting. Exaggerate the process by posting a list of what you want to happen in an obvious location where you and everyone else can see it—on a wall, ceiling, floor, etc. As long as your method works for you, don't worry about being too creative or off-the-wall. What really matters is the outcome of the process.

In the previous chapter, the project example was a trip to Europe. To define success for this project in terms of Time, Cost and Performance, your goals may look like the following:

Time:	June
Budget/Cost:	Up to $10,000 for 2 people
Performance:	Tour Scandinavia

Although you may have a clear picture of what your goal is, someone on the outside looking in needs more information to better understand your expectations. In this case, your travel consultants would be considered your support staff. How could they help you reach your goals without knowing more about your project? For example:

- How long do you want to spend there? Is one day long enough? One week?
- What if your travel agent could get a better deal for you at the end of May?
- Which Scandinavian countries do you want to visit? One? Two? All of them?
- Do you want to add extra excursions to your tour?
- Do you prefer economy accommodations or deluxe?
- Does the $10,000 include all meals, airfare and side trips?
- How flexible are you on your budget? Would $12,000 be a deal breaker?

Having the answers from the person defining success might reveal the following definition of success in greater detail:

Time:	Two to three weeks during the time frame from the last week in May thru June
Budget/Cost:	$10,000 for 2 people, but possibly willing to spend more
Performance:	Tour Norway, Finland, Denmark, Sweden and St. Petersburg, Russia

With a clearer picture in hand, the travel agent can now effectively fulfill the client's expectations. Similarly, any project can be defined using the same technique of asking the right questions before proceeding, thus making better use of precious time.

Pick a project that you are either working on now or plan to work on soon and list the specifics, defining your project in terms of Time, Cost and Performance. What do you know about each?

Time: _____

Budget/Cost: _____

Performance: _____

Who Do You Need to Please? Who Will Accept the Project as Being Successful?

Even though you and your project team may think you're headed in the right direction, in order to ensure success, you need to know who will sign off on your project at the end. It is unacceptable to wait until the project is finished to determine whether or not it is successful. Beginning with the end in mind means not only planning the success of your project, but also getting your plan approved and obtaining a written agreement from the beginning—before you commence implementation.

The person or group defining success and signing off on the project at its conclusion has the power to decide what success means. Their reasoning may or may not make sense to you. That person may be your client or upper management. Your job is to figure out what is needed to please them and negotiate with the appropriate individuals so that your project is considered to be realistic.

Know What Is Most Important and Least Important

For any project, one of the triple constraints will be more important than the others and one will be least important. It is imprudent to ask this question directly, however, as you may be perceived as lacking confidence in the success of your project. There is an old project management saying about Time, Cost and Performance: "Which two do you want? You can't have all three." In reality, you can't ask this question because you know the answer will be: "We want all three."

The best way to approach the subject is when you are in the "anticipating obstacles mode" which will be discussed in more detail in the next chapter. Use the phrase "What do you want us to do if _____ happens?" Fill in the blank, relating it to your project. The answer to this question and other questions related to potential obstacles will filter out what is most important (also known as the Driver of your project) and what is least important, at least for the time being. These factors could change as the project proceeds, but agreeing on which is least important provides you with vital information so that you know what action to take when a problem arises. Unless you follow this procedure, you may find yourself spending more money, extending your end date or reducing the performance specification of your final deliverables.

Again, taking the example of the trip to Scandinavia, asking a few more questions will flush out which constraint is the Driver and which is the weakest constraint. Below are some typical questions to help the process:

- What if the trip costs more than $12,000? Would you prefer to spend less time in each country or visit fewer places? Would it be acceptable if the trip to St. Petersburg were eliminated?

- What if you could get a great package deal for just under $10,000 for three weeks in June, but the accommodations were outside the major cities, not deluxe and no meals except breakfast were included? If this were an option, what would you like to do?

- What if you could visit every place that is listed for under $12,000, but you could only stay 10 days? Would that be okay?

There are other questions and scenarios, but this is how you determine which of the Triple Constraints is most important and which is least important. Ascertaining these constraints will help everyone involved know how to handle problems as they arise during the project. Each person will know whether to spend more money, take more or less time or reduce the quality of the trip.

Asking questions and anticipating obstacles is not a negative activity. Anticipating obstacles and posing questions shows that you are proactive about how you plan to handle potential problems, which is far better than being blindsided by them once they arise.

Know What Is Good Enough

Be aware of what flexibility you have, in terms of Time, Cost and Performance, that will enable you to attain success. For example, you may have a finish date, but how rigid is it? Can you still be successful if you find it necessary to break the project down into stages and complete each stage at different times? Is this satisfactory? How much flexibility exists within your budget? Is it acceptable to be 10% over budget and still be successful or is your budget set in stone? Can you accomplish success at the finish line by eliminating some of the "bells and whistles" in your deliverable?

When managing and working on a project, no one expects you to have all the answers, but asking the right questions is imperative. Brainstorming various options to overcome possible obstacles will help you complete your first-rate project on time, within budget and to spec.

Once you have the Time, Cost and Performance defined in writing, ask for approval from the right person or group—your client. Basically you are throwing the ball back into your client's court, asking: "Is this what you want?" Now is the time to find out if you need to make any adjustments.

But They Don't Know What They Want

You may be thinking, "More often than not, I find that the people I'm trying to please don't really know what they want." Sometimes you may encounter customers, clients and upper management that can't articulate what they want but know it when they see it. Consider this challenge an opportunity to shape the project into what it should be. Be upfront when defining success and document all the unknowns, indicating that your project may, in effect, be a feasibility study to help everyone decide what needs to be done for the "actual" project that follows. In some cases, the final result of your project may be that the project is not feasible and is cancelled or shelved for later. This may seem like a waste of time, but when you or someone else requests a cutting-edge or research-type project for the first time, there will be numerous unknowns. This is the nature of the business. Accept it, build in appropriate contingencies and be sure to document these facts with a positive attitude. Part of your job may be to help people find out what they really want. Think of it as job security.

Document Changes

Change is a certainty. But recurring changes could cause the scope of your project to increase. This is often referred to as "Scope Creep." What may seem like a small change to you and others may snowball into numerous small changes that, added together, could potentially cause your project to run over budget or be delivered later than planned.

Rule of Thumb: When one thing changes, it changes other things.

Decide early on how you will adapt to such changes. Use a "Change Order" form, describing the change and how it will affect the other constraints. For example, if your client wants to add a feature to the project deliverable, document specifically what the change entails and estimate how much it will add to the cost and time of the project. Then obtain approval in writing and renegotiate and revise the terms of the contract with your client as required. Likewise, if the time or cost changes, evaluate how it will influence the other constraints. It's all about Time, Cost and Performance.

Adopt an "I Can Do" Attitude

Instead of telling a customer, client or upper management that you can't do what they want, tell them what you can do. For example, if they ask for a change in the deliverable (Performance), answer, "Yes, I can do that." Then let them know how the Time and Cost will change. Always do your homework to determine the effects of the change, remembering Time, Cost and Performance. When one of these factors changes, look to see how it affects the others.

If you are asked to finish your project sooner, tell your client how this change (Time) affects the deliverable (Performance) and the budget (Cost). Normally, additional resources are required in order to complete a project earlier than the established time. This is referred to as "Crashing the Project."

Agree on how changes will be communicated (e.g., marked-up drawings, revised documents, etc.). Clearly indicate the changes so others can identify them easily.

Let people know what you want them to do by adopting an "I can do" attitude and communicating in a friendly, straightforward manner.

Keep a Log, Diary or Journal for Each Project

Consider keeping a log, diary or journal for each project. Each day, note significant events. What went well? What went awry? This works well for some people, while for others it simply gets in their way, causing too much paperwork. But writing things down in your journal gives you time to focus on and appreciate what is important and what is less significant, reinforces what is going well, sheds light on slip-ups and provides insight into where and how to make improvements.

Your journal may include details that may not be found on your calendar, planner, computer or other organizational devices. No matter what high-tech devices you have at your disposal, never discount the power of recording notes and observations in your own handwriting, even if you enter them into a more sophisticated system later on.

Throw a Project Kick-off Party

Why wait to celebrate? Start your project off on the right foot and throw a Project Kick-off Party. Fire up your project team and energize them from the get-go. If your team members tend to be challenged or unproductive when it comes to getting projects done on time, within budget and/or to the desired quality, it's time to shake things up and make some changes; otherwise, you will continue to get the same results. A Kick-off Party can send a signal that this project is going to be different, in a positive way. Ask everyone to take turns introducing themselves to the team, relating what experience they bring to the table and committing to do their best. Use the opportunity to electrify each other and delight in the experience.

Quick Tips on Jump-starting Your Project

- Know why the project is needed
- Define success in terms of Time, Cost and Performance
- Visualize your deliverable
- Get a reality check
- Put things in writing
- Use the SMART test for goals
- Know what you want and why
- Know who you need to please
- Know what's good enough
- Document all changes
- Have an "I Can Do" attitude
- Keep a project log or journal
- Throw a Project Kick-off Party

Chapter 3:

What Can Hinder Your Success?

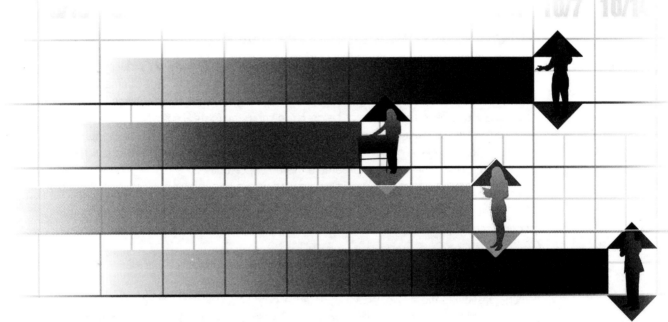

Now that you have defined success in terms of Time, Cost and Performance, you are ready to transition into the Planning phase of your project. This is considered to be a transition since it commences in the latter part of the Definition phase. If the transition has not occurred yet, it needs to become part of your Planning phase; otherwise, the potholes on your road to a successful project will slow you down or cause occasional stoppages to make repairs, costing you more than you ever expected.

Thinking ahead about potential problems saves time later in your project, allowing you to build contingencies into your schedule and budget. Be proactive and take time to identify potential solutions for each possible problem. Ask yourself: "How will I know if a problem occurs?" Then ask: "What is the solution?" And finally: "How will I carry it out?"

Anticipate Obstacles and Solve Problems

Things happen. No matter how much you plan ahead, challenges likely will surface. There are risks to consider. Even if you have done the same type of project dozens of times before, confidence may lead to complacency and, perhaps, mistakes. Have you ever taken a trip to a place you've been to many times before? You know the route like the back of your hand, but while you were focused on something else, you missed a turn. Similar events can occur on your projects. A missed exit on the interstate can cause you to be late, costing you additional money in fuel and possibly even a missed opportunity.

Once you have identified your project and taken the time to define what success means, ask, "What can get in the way of our getting our project done on time, within budget and of good enough quality?"

Ask Open-ended Questions

When questioning those involved about potential problems, pay close attention to your choice of words. For example, take the question: "Are there any problems?" Most people will simply respond, "No." They may have had something in mind to tell you, but they held back. Ask open-ended questions like, "What problems do you foresee?" When a simple one-word response will not suffice, people are usually more inclined to engage in dialogue. Using this approach will provide you with the valuable information you need.

Even if you think you know all the answers, ask open-ended questions of others who are associated with your project and performing part of the work for you, including support people. The more other people who work with you feel involved with your project, the more they will buy into it, feel empowered and be committed. Chances are they will notice things that you might have missed. As you did in the Definition phase, seek a fresh perspective from someone unfamiliar with your project. Even people you may regard as inexperienced can offer helpful input from their own unique perspectives. Respect the feedback of everyone and then make your own decision on how to proceed.

What if you were planning a trip to Terre Haute, Indiana, to represent your company at an important regional meeting where various associates, upper management and key clients will be in attendance? You are responsible for delivering a presentation to inform everyone about the status of a project that affects them. Assume you came up with the definition of success as follows:

Time:	The meeting is March 20 and 21. You are scheduled for a presentation at 1:00 p.m. on March 20.
Cost:	Whatever you can justify within the travel policies of your department, organization and budget of your project.
Performance:	Representing your project to the best of your ability.

As you begin the "What can get in my way?" phase, you may find yourself adding things to help clarify your definition. As you determine what these are, revise your definition accordingly.

- **Time:** What possible things can hinder you from achieving success? You may come up with the following: If you fly to the meeting and leave on March 20, a flight delay or cancellation may cause you to miss your 1 p.m. presentation. Once you identify an obstacle that could possibly happen, ask what you can do to mitigate that problem to ensure your success. Some of the possible solutions for the example above may include taking a flight the day before or driving there instead of flying.

- **Cost:** What possible things can get in your way? What if there is a cost-savings policy, creating a freeze on travel, making it impractical for you to attend in person? Can you send a report to be distributed at the meeting or can someone else make your presentation? Will any of these solutions cause you to spend more money?

- **Performance:** What possible obstacles keep you from achieving success? What if you don't present the information your audience wants? What if they ask questions that you didn't anticipate? What if you forget to bring your audio-visual presentation or the equipment doesn't work? Do you have a backup plan?

Select one of your current or upcoming projects and brainstorm possible obstacles that could get in the way of achieving success. List the possible obstacles in the left column below. In the right column, list potential solutions to each potential problem. Then brainstorm other possible solutions for each problem. Include everyone who is involved with your project; they may have solutions that never occurred to you. As you facilitate this process, keep asking, "What else can we do to solve this problem?" Continue asking "What else?" until a minimum of 10 seconds has elapsed. Then pose the question again. Being proactive and applying this process can help identify potential problems and stimulate the problem-solving process, saving you valuable time later on. This is an example of the principle "Pay me now or pay me later."

Potential obstacles: **Potential solutions:**

_____   _____

_____   _____

_____   _____

Once you have identified the potential obstacles and solutions, you have options to consider when estimating your time and cost as you continue the planning process. Instead of padding or fudging your estimates, you will be able to build in contingencies based on reasons—a definite advantage over guessing.

Now that you have defined success and brainstormed possible obstacles, you are ready to advance to the next phase of planning—creating visuals such as the Work Breakdown Structure (WBS), Network Diagram and Timeline. These will help everyone see that the project depends on their activities being completed in order for the project to move forward.

Quick Tips on Things That Can Get in Your Way

- Anticipate obstacles that could cause delay, overrun your budget or cause the quality to be compromised

- Ask open-ended questions

- Brainstorm possible solutions to mitigate risks and anticipate problems

- Build in contingencies with reasons

- Involve and empower every appropriate person to instill buy-in and commitment

- Value the input of everyone

Step #1 for "Recovering" Project Managers:
Admit when your project has become uncontrollable and unmanageable.

Chapter 4:

Work Your Plan, One Bite at a Time

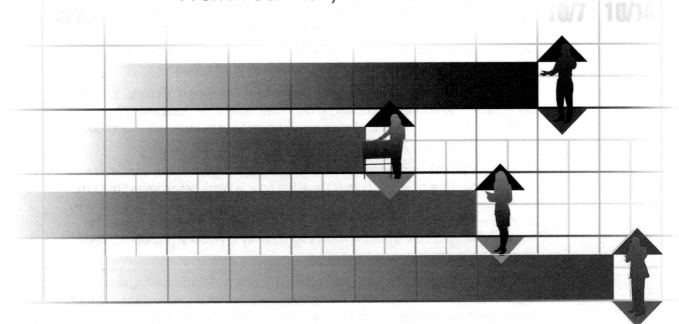

You might be thinking to yourself, "We're already on Chapter 4 and we still haven't started working on our project." Although we have not yet begun implementing the project, this groundwork is essential; otherwise, you may find yourself ahead of schedule but doing the wrong thing.

People with years of project experience will sometimes admit that, even though they don't always have sufficient time to do a project right, they somehow manage to have time to go back and do it over again when the outcome is unacceptable.

Often, a client, customer or upper management may require a project to commence before success is defined. Sometimes these requirements are simply perceived. Your responsibility is to help others comprehend your need to know what success means before moving forward, and to encourage them to understand how this definition applies to your project.

Now that you have evaluated the obstacles that can get in your way, you are ready to brainstorm what actually needs to be done, or the **how** of your project.

The saying "How do you eat an elephant?" applies here. The answer, of course, is: "One bite at a time." Sometimes people don't know where to start. Step back and look at your project and then plan an organized approach. The first step is to break your project down into bite-sized pieces, steps, work packages or sub-units.

What do you and others need to do? What tasks and activities need to be completed from the beginning of the project to its end? This is known as a **Work Breakdown Structure**, often referred to as the **WBS**. Although you are defining the tasks and activities that need to be done in this phase, you do not need to be concerned with the logical order at this time. For now, ignore the sequence. Allow your creativity to flow and brainstorm without restraint. This is referred to as a "brain dump."

What if you, as a volunteer at your local hospital (a not-for-profit organization), discover the hospital wants the newest cutting-edge equipment that could save lives and give them an advantage over competing hospitals in the area? The problem is that each device costs $10,000 and 10 of them are desired, but there is no approved budget for this equipment.

Suppose you come up with the brilliant idea that they should have a silent auction to raise the money and you happen to mention this to the director of the department where you volunteer. Now imagine that, to your amazement, they overwhelmingly love your idea and they elect you to begin working on the project immediately.

Although you thought the silent auction was a great idea, your goal certainly was not to "own" the project. Now, suddenly you are a project manager—and a volunteer project manager in the bargain. Being a respectable, charitable person, you reluctantly agree.

Your volunteer coordinator recruits other volunteers to help you, so you now have your project team. Since you did not select your project team members based on the skills you need, it's important to evaluate what skill sets they possess and then ask for other individuals as you identify your needs. Involving everyone in the process will help you identify all the tasks and activities you must accomplish before achieving your goal—raising $100,000 via a silent auction.

Invite everyone to come to a brainstorming meeting. Ask them to come prepared with a list of things they think will be necessary to accomplish the project. As you and your team members brainstorm together, assign someone to compile a master list as each person shares the tasks and activities they think of. Keep it simple yet meaningful by using keywords to identify each task.

The person recording these tasks can make a list on paper or record each one on a separate sticky note, using bold marking pens to identify the tasks. Add creativity and more visual information by using assorted colors of sticky notes and marking pens. Keep everyone involved, sharing their ideas. This will stimulate the group to think of other tasks that you might have forgotten. If anyone mentions something that seems ridiculous or off-the-wall, recognize this as an integral part of the creative process. Avoid scrutinizing or passing judgment on any idea. Allow the creative process to flow freely.

As you list the tasks, place them in categories according to type of assignment, person doing the work, associated department or whatever makes sense to you. For example, a major project might be broken down into the following sections:

- Design
- Construction
- Start-up
- Follow-up

Within each of these sections might be an additional breakdown by discipline of work, such as:

- Structural
- Equipment
- Piping
- Electrical

It sometimes is advisable to avoid assigning categories to the tasks, but rather to allow the creative process to continue.

Let's say your brainstorming identified some of the following tasks for the silent auction project:

- Prepare letter to businesses
- Send letters
- Decide on location
- Pick a date
- Approve budget
- Approve plan
- Determine businesses to target
- Make a proposal
- Advertise
- Ticket sales
- Food and drinks
- Collect money
- Pick up donations
- Public relations
- Media coverage

Notice there is no logical order for the tasks above. You may be thinking that some of them could be combined and others need to be broken down further. There is no right or wrong way to proceed. The rule of thumb is to identify your tasks at the highest level that communicates good enough information to your group and others involved. This higher level of tasks and activities may be referred to as a Work Package, meaning that there are many other detailed activities that need to occur in order to make the task or work package happen. Don't worry about defining a task, activity or work package. As long as people working on your projects are clear about what they need to do and feel like they are a part of the team, the terms may, in effect, be used interchangeably without causing difficulty.

As you and your team continue the brainstorming process of identifying the tasks, keep in mind the intermediate deliverables that need to be produced during the project. For example, in the Public Relations task, several intermediate tasks may also exist, such as preparing a press release, identifying appropriate media and sending out press releases.

How Much Detail Is Needed?

Even though you may not find it necessary to break things down in finer detail, the people who actually are doing the work may prefer to break their work down to the degree that best suits their needs.

As you and your project team move forward, you may find tasks and activities that either do not need to be done or that can be combined with other tasks. When it is understood that a particular task is part of another task, it does not need to be broken down to that degree of detail.

Demanding that someone break down their tasks to the degree they perceive as busywork does not empower others and can be viewed as micromanaging. Instead, empower the individuals who are doing the work to figure out the best way to carry it out. Provided they deliver their piece of the action on time, within budget and to the expected quality—trust them and allow everyone to do their best.

Select one of your current or upcoming projects and brainstorm the tasks, activities and work packages that you will need to accomplish in order to get your project done successfully:

_____

_____

_____

_____

As you develop your WBS, think about milestones that are meaningful to everyone associated with your project to stimulate buy-in, agreement and empowerment. Include your:

- Project team members
- Support staff
- Client
- Customers
- Users
- Upper management

Typically Forgotten Tasks

Remember to include the following tasks that are often overlooked and can cause missed deadlines, a budget overrun and/or the inability to meet the performance specification:

- Approvals
- Reviews
- Testing
- Prototype or model
- Documentation
- Vendor activities

Just because someone else is responsible for a task does not mean you can't be held accountable for it. Include all activities that need to be done on your project, no matter who is responsible for them. If the success of your project depends on it, it is your responsibility to ensure that it makes its target. Placing blame on someone else is a negative activity, so anticipate the obstacles that can get in your way and be proactive to avoid as many of them as possible.

Looking at past experiences, what are some of the things that went unnoticed by you and your team that caused a problem later in the project? Note them below. Keep a list to use as a reminder not to repeat the same mistakes.

_____

_____

_____

_____

Delegate Creatively

As you identify tasks, begin thinking about who will carry them out. A major complaint of people working on projects is that "There's no one to delegate to." Is this really true? Are you actually doing it all alone? Who are you depending on for the success of your project? Who can help?

Ask for help. Empower yourself by suggesting someone who can lend a hand—someone who can perform specific tasks that they prefer, are good at or want to learn to do better. Whenever possible, make sure the tasks are in alignment with each person's goals and in agreement with the person's supervision. This may not always be possible, but the more alignment you create, the more the person will be motivated to excel.

Consider the following individuals or groups that you may be depending on for the success of your project:

- Vendors
- Legal
- Safety
- Purchasing
- Management
- Engineering
- Information technology
- Research

While you consider whom you are reliant on, look for ways to use the talents and skills of these individuals or groups for the betterment of the project and your organization. Ask and you shall receive.

Whom do you depend on to get your projects done successfully?

_____

_____

_____

As you look at the list you created on the previous page, ask yourself and your team members to brainstorm how those who were identified can do more to help complete your project on schedule, within budget and to the desired quality. Write your results in the left column below. To the right of each item, note one or more actions that you can take to make each one happen. Then take the appropriate action.

Desired results: **Actions to accomplish:**

_____   _____

_____   _____

_____   _____

Quick Tips on Working Your Plan

- Plan your project before implementing it
- Practice your project management skills by volunteering for a nonprofit group
- Use a WBS for your personal projects as well as projects at work
- Involve everyone associated with and affected by your project
- Allow your creativity to flow freely. The logic will happen later.
- Color-code to add a more visual impact
- Make your WBS appropriate to the complexity and length of your project and the expertise of your team
- Be alert for others who can help
- Ask for help from those who have the skill-sets you need
- Learn from past mistakes
- Delegate creatively

Chapter 5:

*The Logic of Your Project—
the Network Diagram*

Prior to establishing the logic of your project, you first defined success in terms of time, cost and performance. Then you moved forward to break it down into bite-sized pieces. Now you're ready to take each of those pieces and place them into logical order, from the beginning of the project to the end.

What Is a Network Diagram?

This logic or sequence of activities of a project is referred to as a **Network Diagram**. It's like a road map for your project. When planning a driving trip, you may get directions from the Internet. Notice that these Web sites provide not only a detailed list of driving directions but also an overview map. Your Network Diagram is the visual overview road map of your project.

Relating project management skills to everyday life helps you to realize that you're already using many of these skills and tools. Sometimes the tools may be written down and formal while at other times, unwritten, verbalized or merely understood and used more casually. This is fine when you have less complex projects that don't involve the interaction of others. Even if you don't end up using a Network Diagram after you commence work on project activities, creating a Network Diagram can be helpful because it allows planning and foresight before the actual work begins.

What if you decided to throw a large dinner party or a project celebration party? If you never did anything like this before, you would benefit by planning the party through the use of a Network Diagram. Let's say you brainstormed a list of actions you would need to perform in order to create a successful party. A few of these activities might include:

- Decide on location
- List guests
- Send invitations
- Gather responses
- Plan menu
- Buy food
- Set up
- Clean up

Although I'm sure you could come up with more tasks than those listed above, let's start by placing them in order, from the beginning to the end of this project.

Place Activities in Sequential Order

Now you're ready to place the activities in order. One of the best methods of preparing the Network Diagram is to place each identified activity on a sticky note. Use a bold marking pen to identify the tasks so that they can be readily seen from a distance. This allows enough room to identify each activity using key words. It isn't necessary to describe the activity in more detail than is needed at this point; write just enough information so you know what the activity means. You may have done this already if you created a work breakdown structure (WBS) for your project.

On more complex work-related projects, try standing up and remaining standing while you're creating the Network Diagram. This stimulates creativity, gets everyone more involved and maintains energy. To facilitate this process, a project team will use flip chart paper placed horizontally on the wall. (To avoid unintentionally marking on the wall itself, use two sheets to create a double thickness.) Each sticky note activity will then be placed on this paper. Depending on the complexity of the project, this could take more paper.

On the left side of the Network Diagram place the activity called "Start" and on the right side place the activity called "Finish." You can devise different names for these two activities as long as everyone can see the beginning and end of the project.

Start						Finish

Next, ask yourself and others involved, "What is the first thing we need to do?" Typically, the answers will vary. Once you start the project, it will be possible to begin more than one activity simultaneously; therefore, you may already find activities that can occur in the same time frame. You also may find that what you initially thought was the first step really shouldn't be. This is a work in progress, so enjoy the process. Placing the activities in logical order helps everyone see other activities that might otherwise have been overlooked in the work breakdown structure.

Be sure to work from left to right, progressing to the project's conclusion. Some people will try to be creative and show their logic from top to bottom, but this often leads to confusion. The safer option is to create a Network Diagram similar to those created by most software programs, since this is something people may be more familiar with.

It is not necessary to start in any particular order. Like with a puzzle, eventually the pieces will all come together. Unlike with a puzzle, there is likely more than one way to get your project done successfully, although some methods may be faster or more cost effective than others.

What Are Predecessors?

Predecessors are activities that need to be done before another activity can start. You can also refer to them as an activity's dependencies.

When considering any activity, ask "Where does this go?" and "What needs to be done in order for this activity to start?" In other words, identify your dependencies. Using the Party project example, let's arbitrarily pick up the sticky note activity called "Buy Everything" and, for now, place it in the middle of the diagram. Ask yourself: "What needs to happen before this can begin?" Obviously, one of the predecessors will be "Plan Menu." As you develop the Network Diagram, usually someone will notice when an activity is placed where it doesn't make sense. This is an excellent example of why it's so important to involve everyone in this process. In this early stage of the project, with everyone on their feet, actively engaged, you are more likely to find problems in your logic.

Placing the remaining activities from your list, you might initially come up with what is shown in the figure on the next page.

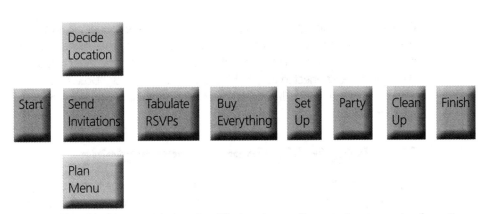

Note: Although this example is a simplified project to illustrate the concepts of creating a Network Diagram, your real-life projects will presumably be more detailed and complex.

Show Connectivity Among Activities

The initial Network Diagram has the activities arranged from left to right to show the flow of the project. However, without lines and arrows connecting them, you can only make assumptions on how each activity is connected to the others. You don't know for certain which activities need to be completed before the others begin.

Consequently your next step is to draw lines connecting every activity. Using a pencil is best because you may need to rearrange the placement of some activities. This is part of the creative process. A distinct benefit of creating the Network Diagram is being able to view the options and to select the most effective ones.

As the project team hovers around the Network Diagram, connect the activities with lines, talk things out, stay alert and listen to everyone's ideas. One person may want to assume the lead, but even though others may have more experience, each individual team member needs to share their ideas and feedback. A less experienced person or someone outside the project may have a fresh perspective or helpful ideas.

Refrain from being negative or excessively critical. Remain assertive and explain your ideas and rationale. Be aware of anyone on the team who seems disconnected. Get everyone directly involved at the outset. You want their buy-in and the benefit of their viewpoints. Also, if anyone has concerns, you need to hear them out at this stage, before they're overheard later in the hallway saying "It'll never work." Flush out as many problems as you can. Then ask for agreement.

Once everyone is in agreement on how the activities are connected, notice if any activity is still not connected. Every activity should have at least one line linking into it as well as out of it except for "Start" and "Finish." If any activity is still not connected, ask "What should this logically be connected to?" If the answer is unclear, ask "Do we need it?" Eventually, a member of the team will remove the activity, combine it with another or connect it to another activity.

Make It Clear, Simple and Understandable

Use arrows to show the connections from left to right in the Network Diagram below to add clarity. Note that all lines connecting the activities move from left to right. Since the Network Diagram represents progress forward in time, it's best to place activities so that the flow is forward, (i.e., no connections point to activities to the left; all arrows must point to the right). Although it is possible to communicate the logic of your project with some lines pointing backward, it tends to make the diagram more complex. The purpose of the Network Diagram is to clearly communicate what needs to be done from the beginning to the end, so that everyone associated with the project can understand the logic and agree on it. Keep it straightforward.

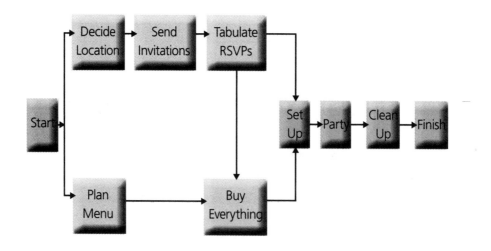

Even though some of the same activities in the previous figure are duplicated here, observe that the location of some of the activities changed to more clearly show the correct path from the beginning of the project to the end. Some of the activity names are abbreviated to accommodate the sticky note.

You will likely make some additional changes to your Network Diagram. Use correction tape, correction fluid or masking tape so that stray lines do not clutter your drawing. Make your Network Diagram clean and presentable enough to show to your client.

Once you are comfortable with the logic, you still have two other bits of information to add to each activity: a reference number at the top left and an estimated duration of time at the top right. The figure below shows the completed Network Diagram, which is considered to be final unless the need to make changes arises.

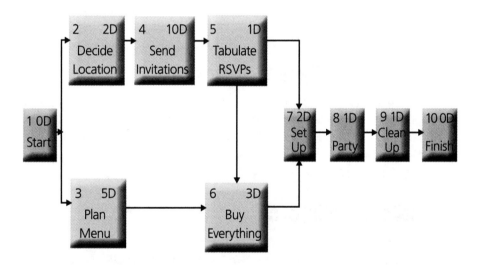

Once you've completed the diagram, it's helpful to ask one of the team members to "talk it through" to the other team members. This run-through allows everyone to take a step back, look and listen to see if what you have decided still makes sense. It is beneficial if the person making this "stand-up presentation" is the one most familiar with the project. Observe the nonverbal cues of the presenter as well as those of the other members of the team. How confident are they in what is being proposed? Do you think this plan will work? This is a good time to challenge the plan and make appropriate changes.

Seek an Outside Opinion

Ask for a second opinion. Solicit someone from outside your project or even outside your company and ask them, "Does this make sense?" Be cautious not to divulge confidential or sensitive information to others without a secrecy agreement.

Revise the Plan and Document Changes

Once the Network Diagram is established and agreed upon, you are ready to work your plan.

Continue to be observant for activities you end up doing that were not included in the initial plan. For example, while in the "Tabulating the RSVPs" activity, if you decide to be more accurate and contact everyone who did not respond, you could add another activity called "Follow-up Invites" so that when you decide to do a similar project in the future, you could add that activity at the beginning. For this reason, record all Network Diagram updates.

Investigate Alternate Approaches

For a fascinating exercise, ask two or more groups to independently create a Network Diagram for the same project. When the groups are finished, observe how each of them tackled the project. Reviewing the pros and cons of the various scenarios that each group comes up with may lead to a new and improved way of implementing the project or, sometimes, even to the discovery of a competitive edge.

Build In Contingency

Even though in the previous steps leading to the Network Diagram you may have asked "What can happen to get in our way?," this is still a good question to continue to ask and contemplate.

Add appropriate activities or extra time to existing activities based on the possible scenarios. The additional time added to a task should be based on the real possibilities that could happen and how likely they are to occur. Document everything, including the extra time you have estimated and why. This shows that you have done your homework.

In the example in the previous figure, two days are shown for "Set Up" and one day for "Party." It may be possible to do both activities on the same day, but if you wait until the day of the party to do the entire set-up, you may run into unexpected problems and little or no time to fix them. Always know what is realistic. It might even be unrealistic to set up two days before. If this is the case, revise the Network Diagram accordingly.

Exercise: Select a project that you have completed, are currently working on or plan to start. Create a Network Diagram using the concepts in this chapter.

Use a Network Diagram for Multiple Projects

Consider all the projects and work packages that you currently are engaged in at work, at home and in your community. Essentially, you are juggling multiple projects. Some examples may include:

- Write procedure for boss

- Finish quality improvement project

- Cost saving evaluation

- Special outing with kids

- Anniversary dinner with spouse

- Prepare presentation for conference in June

- Home improvement: Finish basement

- Certification in project management

- Continuing education credits

- Silent auction for school

- Prepare and file taxes

- Business trip to New York

- Vacation in Hawaii

Use a Network Diagram to track any or all of these tasks. Using the list above as an example, the "Prepare presentation" activity may need to be finished by a certain date and before the "Business trip to New York." Therefore the "Business trip" activity is dependent on finishing the "Prepare Presentation" activity. Many of these projects may be occurring concurrently and should be shown as such on the Network Diagram.

Exercise: List all the projects you currently are working on and those that you anticipate in the near future. Next, place each on a sticky note and create your own customized Network Diagram, showing any activity that needs to be done before another, as well as those that can happen concurrently. Post them on the wall of your office so that they are visible to you and to others. When someone gives you a new project, it's easier to see where it fits in best. This also allows those responsible for assigning you more work an opportunity to see your workload in perspective. The visual presents an opportunity to communicate with others about what projects and activities are most important, which ones should be delayed and which ones can possibly be reassigned to others.

> The nice thing about not planning is that failure comes as a complete surprise rather than being preceded by a period of worry and depression.

Quick Tips on Network Diagrams

- Stand while creating a diagram to stimulate creativity
- Involve all key players
- Use a sticky note and clearly label each activity using key words
- Work from left to right, showing flow of project from start to finish
- Use lines and arrows to show connectivity
- Number each activity to ease identification and reference
- Estimate duration of time for each activity and add to each
- Make diagram neat and legible enough to present in a meeting
- Ask for an outside opinion to ensure it makes sense
- Apply the Network Diagram process at work and at home

Chapter 6:

Time Is Money

Now that you have defined success, created your WBS and produced your Network Diagram, you are ready to add the time dimension to your plan. "But it isn't necessary to estimate time," you may be thinking to yourself. "Someone else has already decided when the project needs to be done."

The finish date was dictated to you and it's up to you to get it done on time, right? Yes and no. You may be responsible for getting your projects done on time, but you also have the added responsibility of making your projects realistic. An impossible project creates tension, stress and lack of motivation. It is counterproductive to stand by and permit this to happen. When you continue doing things the same way, you can expect the same results. Take positive action. Practice good leadership skills even if you don't consider yourself to be a leader. Most people will respect you for it.

> "The definition of insanity is doing the same thing over and over and expecting different results."
>
> — *Benjamin Franklin*

Empower Yourself to Make Projects Realistic

The finish date of your project may have been dictated to you; nevertheless it is up to you to see that your project is realistic rather than impossible. When your timeline seems impossible, it's time to do your homework. Get the facts. Gather the details and document *why* you will need more time or more money or both to complete the project.

Fudging and padding your project are negative terms for building in contingency. The key is to factor in contingency for your project based on potential problems. Estimate the additional time and cost in the event those obstacles occur. If you arbitrarily fudge or pad your project's schedule and cost in excess of what would be considered within reason, you may wind up with estimates that are unbelievable.

Although you may get your current project done on time and within budget, others may not believe your future estimates. Consequently, strive for realistic estimates based on specific foreseeable obstacles. Building in 10% is acceptable for most projects to account for unexpected costs and delays. When what you are requesting makes sense and you have it in writing, you are more likely to get the resources you need. Use the SMART approach. Explain the situation in specific, concrete terms. Then ask for what you want and need to make the project realistic. You only get something when you ask for it.

This may require the support of the next level of management, so be sure to follow the appropriate chain of command. Be assertive, not aggressive. Complaining about an impossible project is a waste of time unless you are complaining to someone who can change the situation.

> "If you are like most people, you may be holding yourself back by not asking for the information, assistance, support, money and time you need to fulfill your vision and make your dreams come true."
>
> — *Jack Canfield,* The Success Principles

Make Your Time Estimates SMART

All too often, projects become stuck, leaving everyone wondering why. Fingers are pointed and blame assigned. When you get down to the basics of Time, Cost and Performance, the answer usually becomes obvious. The chief reasons why projects are not finished on time are: The time element was never defined, it was ignored or it was unrealistic.

Ask the question "When do you want the project to be finished?" When the answer is "Well, we don't know for sure," you're getting the defined result—an indefinite date. Remember the SMART acronym. Although the "T" stands for Time, the "SMAR" parts of this acronym also apply. The Time needs to be Specific, Measurable, Agreed-upon and Realistic.

In addition to defining a SMART end date for your projects, you need to have SMART time estimates for the duration of each task, activity and work package. Each sticky note on your Network Diagram needs to have a duration of time associated with it. In addition to duration and dependencies to determine when an activity starts, for various reasons pertinent to your project, some tasks might have specific start or finish dates associated with them. Include these fixed dates in your timeline.

Estimate Duration of Time as Well as Actual Time

When you estimate the time for each task, estimate the duration of time or calendar time from the beginning of the task to the end of it. In the previous chapter, the example project had a "Plan Menu" task, which had an estimated duration of five days. This doesn't necessarily mean that someone will work on that task full-time for five days. It could be that the task only takes a total of four hours to complete, but those four hours may need to happen at intervals over a course of five days. Therefore, the duration of time estimate is five days.

Those four hours might involve more than one person working on the task. Bear in mind that you estimated the "Plan Menu" task to be four hours so that, later on, you could see how accurate your estimate turned out to be. Even though a book may take a total of 10 hours to read, it may take you 10 days, over time, to complete the activity. Instead of asking "How long will the tasks take?," a more precise question would be "When can you have this task completed?"

Involve the People Actually Doing the Work

When you have others working on your project, rather than telling them which tasks you want them to do, ask them which tasks they need to do in order to obtain the desired result for a successful project. This approach is more empowering and helps create buy-in and commitment.

Those who are actually doing the work know best what is needed and how long it should take. These other people are often working on your project on a part-time basis and may be referred to as "ad hoc personnel," "support staff" or "part-time resources." Remember that people you are depending on almost certainly have other projects and people to satisfy, so consider them as "shared resources." Even though you may need 10 hours of time for your project from one of your shared resources, the actual duration may take 10 days due to reasons such as other projects awaiting approvals and other tasks to be completed.

You are responsible for getting your part of the project completed successfully and yet you are dependent upon your support staff. Since you want to encourage buy-in and commitment, empower others to provide you with their best estimate of time duration and actual hours; take into account, however, that your job also entails asking the right questions.

Frequently, these ad hoc personnel do not report to you; they may even be from outside your department or your company. Therefore, although you may not have the authority to tell them what to do, you do have an obligation to let them know what needs to be done. This is where the "A" component of the SMART acronym (Agreed-upon) comes in. Do not expect people to do anything for you unless they first agree to do it.

Ask the Right Questions

When you empower others to give you a time approximation for their work, it is essential to keep the information straight. When you pose the question "How long will each task take?" listen carefully and then follow up with another question: "What obstacles could delay this task?" Pay attention and record the responses.

Next ask "If these problems crop up, how long will this task take?" Record this as your pessimistic or longest time estimate for this task.

Then pose the question "If everything goes well, how long will this task take?" Note this as your optimistic or shortest time estimate for this task.

Your final query should be "In your opinion, how much time is this task likely to take?" Record this. In all likelihood, this will be your estimate, since it takes into consideration some of the delays that might occur and yet remains realistic because of built-in contingency time. This is referred to as the most likely or realistic time estimate.

Consider Who Will Do the Work

When estimating the time allotted for each task, be sure to consider who will be assigned to perform it. Consider how likely it is that the person doing the work will be well organized, work rapidly and have the most experience in order to complete the task on schedule and to the quality desired. Time, Cost and Performance are the heart and soul of managing projects—the main reason why these three important stages of project management keep popping up.

Of the questions mentioned above, another might be: "Who will do this task?" What if you don't get the experience level that you expected? In this instance, how long will the task require? Does the person have the skills you need or did you just acquire another warm body? If the person added to your project does not have the skills or desire to do what is needed, your task and perhaps even your project may be delayed. What about other resources of support personnel and equipment? Will they be available when you need them? How realistic are your expectations? Are they a wish, a hope, a dream? Or are they based on reality?

Track Your Past Experiences

Despite the fact that an estimate based on gut feeling may not be viewed by others with confidence, there will be times when that is all you have to go on. One of the best methods to gain more experience for future estimates is to track them. Once the task is completed, note the length of time the task actually took. On a large and complicated project, this could be a daunting undertaking. Tracking tasks that have a greater likelihood of being repeated in the future will give you the greatest payback. Don't be concerned about inadvertently omitting or overlooking something; just begin the process of recording what you think is most important and add additional tasks as you discover them.

Use a spreadsheet to gather the information. In the far-left column, use keywords to identify your tasks. In the second column note the estimated time and in the third column show your actual time. Below is an example based on the sample project from the last chapter indicating actual times.

Task	Estimated Time (days)	Actual Time (days)
Decide Location	2	3
Send Invitations	10	7
Plan Menu	5	6
Tabulate RSVPs	1	1
Buy Everything	3	3
Set Up	2	1
Party	1	1
Clean Up	1	2

It is easier to search for keywords to better observe your historical estimates and actual times once you have set up your spreadsheet on your computer. You can then decide your future estimates relative to the complexity of your future projects.

Improve Your Track Record

What percentage of your projects get done on time or sooner? If you don't know the answer, or if you don't have facts to substantiate this, research the data and analyze the results. This can be a predictor of the odds of getting your current and future projects done on time. Unless you change the way you are doing things, you will continue to get the same results.

What percentage of your projects get done on time or sooner? _____

What is your short-term goal to make your percentage higher? _____

What is your long-term goal to make your percentage higher? _____

Make a commitment and strive for continual improvement.

Select one of your current or upcoming projects and brainstorm how you can get your project done on time or ahead of schedule. Ask everyone associated with the project.

_____

_____

_____

_____

Activities Typically Forgotten When Estimating Time

As you did for the WBS, consider some things that you might otherwise have forgotten or ignored. Include them in your time estimates when appropriate. Then go back and incorporate anything you missed into your WBS and Network Diagram. You might not want to include some of them as separate tasks.

For example, a weekly meeting may not be necessary to include as a separate task, but a review meeting with your client, customer or outside vendor could prove to be more time-consuming and identifiable. In such cases, consider adding it as a specific task.

Remember to include the following tasks that often are overlooked, causing projects to miss their deadlines:

- Travel
- Major reviews
- Audits
- Testing
- Quality assurance
- Training
- Prototype or model
- Documentation, policies, procedures and manuals
- As-built drawings
- Vendor activities
- Final inspection or hand-off
- Identification of major milestones important to others

Think about your past projects. What other tasks and activities could you have included in those projects to keep them on track? As you implement your project, make a checklist of things that you initially missed that you need to remember in the future. This may be something to include in your project log, journal or diary, but it is also advantageous to have it handy to help you avoid making the same or similar mistakes in the future.

Below, list the items that you and your project team need to include in future Work Breakdown Structures and Network Diagrams so you can include them in your time estimates:

_____

_____

_____

_____

Keep Track of Hours Spent

Typically, contractors, engineers, construction personnel and others working on major projects will input the number of hours spent on each project. This serves a dual purpose: It helps the project manager keep the project budget under control and records the actual number of hours so that future estimates can be based on this experience.

As more people and organizations continue to refer to their work as projects, not everyone uses all of the project management tools. Many organizations do not track the number of hours that people spend on projects. Although this may help the bottom line of the company, an increasing number of people working under these conditions are working more overtime than they would like and taking work home.

Track the number of hours you spend on each project, even if monitoring it isn't required. This information will help you keep things in perspective. It also will allow you to develop the discipline for a time when you are responsible for keeping track of the time and cost of a project.

Too often when project personnel admit that their company doesn't track the hours spent, they realize that it is costing someone time and money—usually themselves. Could that be one of the reasons why some companies aren't doing as well as their competition? This is something to at least consider.

Typical cost components include:

- Labor
- Overhead
- Incentives
- Materials
- Supplies

Estimate the Cost of Materials and Supplies

In addition to the cost of people working on your projects, there are the added expenditures for materials and supplies. As previously mentioned, some project managers may not deem the tracking of costs to be significant, including the cost of the materials and supplies. If your corporation falls into this category, the fact that you don't have to concern yourself with these details may seem beneficial. But keep in mind that an essential responsibility of a project manager is being accountable for the costs of a project.

Tracking costs, even if it isn't required by your company, is always a prudent practice. Implementing exceptional project management skills will undoubtedly help you on future projects as well as in other organizations.

If you were planning a project to enhance your home or your own business, would you track the costs? Of course. You would begin by getting estimates and quotes on anticipated costs of materials and supplies in writing.

Consider landscaping or removing trees from your property to be projects, even if you contracted the work to someone else. Would you have a large tree removed from your property without getting an estimate? Presumably you would obtain more than one estimate and evaluate not only the cost, but the time the contractor would take to accomplish your job. You would also evaluate the quality of their proposed work.

Act as if the projects at work are your own; be responsible for the quality, cost and time. Even if you do not have the title or responsibility of a project manager, you can still practice and sharpen your skills for future endeavors. In all likelihood, you've already recognized the need for these skills and are using them intuitively in your everyday life.

Be aware of the potential projects that exist right under your nose. You may never see the world the same way again.

Quick Tips on Time and Cost

- Avoid creating the impossible job

- Empower yourself to make time estimates SMART

- Estimate time duration, keeping in mind actual hours

- Involve the people actually doing the work, including shared resources

- Consider what can delay each task and build in contingency time

- Establish who will do the work; who has the skills needed

- Do not expect people to do anything for you unless they agree to it. ASK.

- Know how frequently you get your projects done on time or ahead of schedule

- Gather data to improve your future estimates

- Track your hours and costs even if it's not required

Chapter 7:

The Timeline (The Gantt Chart)

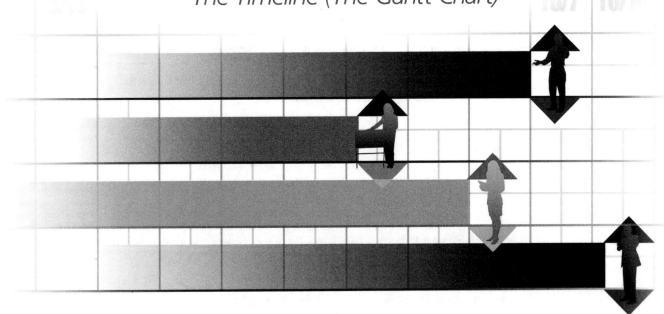

Now that you have defined success, created your WBS, produced your Network Diagram and added the time dimension, you're ready to create the visual of a real timeline, showing when each task is scheduled to happen.

Plan your work, work your plan.

In the 1910s, Henry Gantt, a mechanical engineer and management consultant, developed a method of creating a timeline diagram that was used on major infrastructure projects, including the Hoover Dam and the modern Interstate highway systems. Withstanding the test of time, the Gantt Chart is still a tried-and-true technique. Today, many project management software applications default to this form of visual timeline.

Gather the Facts—Create the Task Table

Whether you use software to generate your timeline or not, your first step is to create a Task Table showing the details for each task, namely the:

- Task name

- Task number

- Dependency number

- Time duration

Refer to the Network Diagram from Chapter 5, shown on the next page. Note that there are 10 tasks, numbered 1 through 10. Each task has a name, dependency and time duration. All you need to do is take this information and fill in the data on a Task Table.

Start by entering the 10 task numbers and 10 task names in the appropriate columns. Next fill in the time duration for each respective task. The last step is to examine each task in order and ask "What needs to be done in order for this task to begin?"

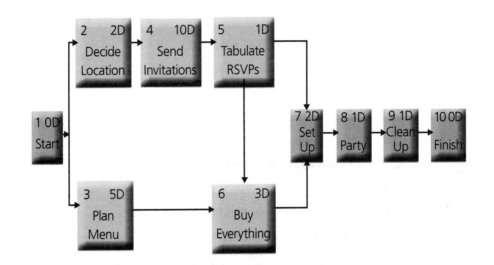

For Task #1, because it is the beginning of the project, the dependency doesn't exist. Task #1 also does not have a time duration. When this occurs, in project management terms it is known as a Dummy Task. Its function is simply to add information.

Next look at Task #2 and ask "What needs to be done in order for this task to begin?" Always look at the task to the left and follow the line or lines to the left. Never look to the right of the task and do not follow any lines that flow to the right. Remember that a timeline always moves forward, as real time does. Therefore, the dependency for Task #2 is Task #1. In other words, the only task that needs to be done in order for Task #2 to begin is Task #1.

Therefore:

- Task #1 is the beginning of your project and not dependent on anything inside your project
- Task #2 can start when Task #1 is finished

Likewise:

- Task #3 can start when Task #1 is finished

- Task #4 can start when Task #2 is finished

- Task #5 can start when Task #4 is finished

- Task #6 can start when Tasks #3 and #5 are finished

- Task #7 can start when Tasks #5 and #6 are finished

- Task #8 can start when Task #7 is finished

- Task #9 can start when Task #8 is finished

- Task #10 can start when Task #9 is finished

The resulting Task Table for the Network Diagram example in Chapter 5 is shown below:

Task #	Task Name	Dependency	Duration Time (days)
1	Start	n/a	0
2	Decide Location	1	2
3	Plan Menu	1	5
4	Send Invitations	2	10
5	Tabulate RSVPs	4	1
6	Buy Everything	3,5	3
7	Set Up	5,6	2
8	Party	7	1
9	Clean Up	8	1
10	Finish	9	0

Note that Tasks #6 and #7 have two dependencies. In order for Task #6 to begin, Tasks #3 and #5 need to be completed.

Similarly, in order for Task #7 to start, Tasks #5 and #6 need to be finished.

Every other task in the example has only one dependent task—the one preceding it, also known as its Predecessor.

You can now use the Task Table data to create the visual of your timeline. This can be done either by hand or by using a computer program such as Microsoft® Project.

In reality, the Task Table is the left side of your Gantt Chart, so by transposing your data you have started your timeline, as shown in Figure 7.1. (*Editor's note:* See page 140 for a sample, reproducible Gantt Chart.)

ID#	Task Name	Duration	Prede-cessors	1	2	3	4	5	6	7	8	9	10	11	12	13	14	15	16	17	18	19	20
1	Start	0	n/a																				
2	Decide Location	2	1																				
3	Plan Menu	5	1																				
4	Send Invitations	10	2																				
5	Tabulate RSVPs	1	4																				
6	Buy Everything	3	3, 5																				
7	Set Up	2	5, 6																				
8	Party	1	7																				
9	Clean Up	1	8																				
10	Finish	0	9																				

Figure 7.1

Create Your Timeline

As you begin to create your timeline, note that each vertical column depicts one increment of time. In this case it is one day; however, the time increment could be shown in weeks, months or hours, depending on your needs.

Sometimes it is more complicated to explain the process on paper than it is to actually see it done. Have you ever read the directions to a board game? The directions are sometimes difficult to comprehend and quite humorous. You may find the same is true in the following description. Actually it sounds more difficult than it is.

To begin, draw an open diamond symbol on the line indicating day #0 for Task #1. This depicts the start of your project as shown on Figure 7.2.

ID#	Task Name	Duration	Prede-cessors	1	2	3	4	5	6	7	8	9	10	11	12	13	14	15	16	17	18	19	20
1	Start	0	n/a	◇																			
2	Decide Location	2	1																				
3	Plan Menu	5	1																				
4	Send Invitations	10	2																				
5	Tabulate RSVPs	1	4																				
6	Buy Everything	3	3, 5																				
7	Set Up	2	5, 6																				
8	Party	1	7																				
9	Clean Up	1	8																				
10	Finish	0	9																				

Figure 7.2

Task #2 is dependent on Task #1 being complete, so it will begin at day #0. Note the open circle shown on Day #0. Since the duration of Task #2 is two days, you would draw an open circle on the line indicating two days (or increments) to the right of day #0. Note the open circle on day #2 across from Task #2. Next connect a line between both circles and you have the timeline for Task #2. Figure 7.3 illustrates this.

Task #3 is next, and you continue in the same fashion. Its dependency is Task #1, so you draw a circle on the line indicating the day that Task #1 is finished, which is day #0. Since the duration of Task #3 is 5 days, you draw an open circle on the line indicating 5 days (or increments) to the right of day #0. Note the open circle on day #5 across from Task #3 in Figure 7.3. After that, connect a line between both circles and you have the timeline for Task #3 as shown in Figure 7.3.

ID#	Task Name	Duration	Prede-cessors	1	2	3	4	5	6	7	8	9	10	11	12	13	14	15	16	17	18	19	20
1	Start	0	n/a	◇																			
2	Decide Location	2	1	○—	—○																		
3	Plan Menu	5	1	○—	—	—	—○																
4	Send Invitations	10	2																				
5	Tabulate RSVPs	1	4																				
6	Buy Everything	3	3, 5																				
7	Set Up	2	5, 6																				
8	Party	1	7																				
9	Clean Up	1	8																				
10	Finish	0	9																				

Figure 7.3

You can already see some benefits of the Gantt Chart. It allows you to look at any particular increment of time and notice what should be happening. This will help you and others stay on track.

Take each task and follow the same procedure as you did above to draw your Gantt Chart for the entire project. Figure 7.4 shows a circle noting the beginning and end of each task and a line connecting both circles, indicating the duration of each task.

ID#	Task Name	Duration	Predecessors	1	2	3	4	5	6	7	8	9	10	11	12	13	14	15	16	17	18	19	20
1	Start	0	n/a	◇																			
2	Decide Location	2	1	○—○																			
3	Plan Menu	5	1	○——————○																			
4	Send Invitations	10	2		○——————————————○																		
5	Tabulate RSVPs	1	4												○—○								
6	Buy Everything	3	3, 5														○——————○						
7	Set Up	2	5, 6																○—○				
8	Party	1	7																		○—○		
9	Clean Up	1	8																			○—○	
10	Finish	0	9																				◇

Figure 7.4

Note that since Task #6 is dependent on more than one task it can't start until both tasks #3 and #5 preceding it are completed. Therefore, Task #6 starts on day #14 since that is when Task #5 is done.

Task #7 is also dependent on two Tasks, #5 and #6, so both tasks must be completed before Task #7 can begin. Figure 7.4 shows Task #7 happening on days #17 and #18.

Show Slack Time or Float Time

Although Figure 7.4 shows all the tasks with lines connected, it may still be unclear to you and others. With the help of some dashed lines and arrows, your timeline can communicate a more complete and simplified picture. In Figure 7.4, notice that Task #3 ends on a day that nothing else appears to begin. Also notice that Task #3 does not need to be completed until Task #6 starts on day #14.

ID#	Task Name	Duration	Prede-cessors	1	2	3	4	5	6	7	8	9	10	11	12	13	14	15	16	17	18	19	20
1	Start	0	n/a																				
2	Decide Location	2	1																				
3	Plan Menu	5	1																				
4	Send Invitations	10	2																				
5	Tabulate RSVPs	1	4																				
6	Buy Everything	3	3, 5																				
7	Set Up	2	5, 6																				
8	Party	1	7																				
9	Clean Up	1	8																				
10	Finish	0	9																				

Figure 7.5

To show this more clearly, Figure 7.5 shows another circle on Task #3 at day #14 and a dashed line connecting the circles between day #6 and day #14. The dashed line shows what is known as float time or slack time, meaning the tasks can be delayed and still allow your project to be done on time.

Add Arrows to Your Gantt Chart

Although the dashed lines show slack or float time, adding arrows and vertical lines makes your visual even more understandable. Figure 7.6 shows these additions so that your Gantt Chart is unmistakably clear.

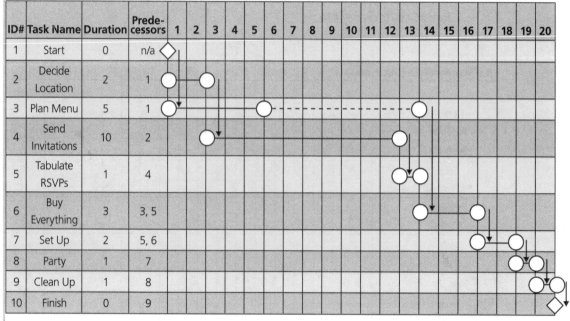

ID#	Task Name	Duration	Prede-cessors	1	2	3	4	5	6	7	8	9	10	11	12	13	14	15	16	17	18	19	20
1	Start	0	n/a																				
2	Decide Location	2	1																				
3	Plan Menu	5	1																				
4	Send Invitations	10	2																				
5	Tabulate RSVPs	1	4																				
6	Buy Everything	3	3, 5																				
7	Set Up	2	5, 6																				
8	Party	1	7																				
9	Clean Up	1	8																				
10	Finish	0	9																				

Figure 7.6

Where Is Your Critical Path?

One of the most important things to know about your project is where your critical path is. All the tasks need to be done on your project, so all the tasks are, in effect, critical because they all must be done. But the critical path refers to the tasks that are on the path that takes the longest time from the beginning of your project to the end. Any delay on that path means that your project will be completed later than planned.

An easy way to manually find your critical path is to work your way backwards from the end of the project to the beginning. In Figure 7.6, notice the dashed line. Any time you have a dashed line that indicates some slack time it means that those tasks are not on the critical path. Starting at the end of your Gantt Chart, follow the lines back to the beginning. As you work your way to the left from Task #10 to Task #6, it's a clear shot with no dashed lines, so all of those tasks are on your critical path.

Task #6 is dependent on Tasks #3 and #5, but since Task #3 shows a dashed line, it is not on the critical path, so follow Task #6 up through Task #4, then on to Task #2, back to the start of your project, Task #1. This is your critical path. Figure 7.7 shows your critical path in bold.

ID#	Task Name	Duration	Prede-cessors	1	2	3	4	5	6	7	8	9	10	11	12	13	14	15	16	17	18	19	20
1	Start	0	n/a	◇																			
2	Decide Location	2	1	○	━	○																	
3	Plan Menu	5	1	○				○	-	-	-	-	-	-	-	-	○						
4	Send Invitations	10	2			○	━	━	━	━	━	━	━	━	━	○							
5	Tabulate RSVPs	1	4													○━○							
6	Buy Everything	3	3, 5															○	━	○			
7	Set Up	2	5, 6																	○	━	○	
8	Party	1	7																			○	○
9	Clean Up	1	8																				○○
10	Finish	0	9																				◇

Figure 7.7

Select one of your current or upcoming projects and create a Task Table and a Timeline (Gantt Chart) based your data. Use the blank Gantt Chart on page 140. Also consider creating your manual Gantt Chart using lined flip chart paper with the lines running vertically and with each space representing a time increment. This method works well when demonstrating an overview of your timeline in a small meeting room or to post on a wall for others to see the progress of your project.

Using Software to Draw Your Timeline

There are many software programs that are useful and powerful tools to automatically draw your Gantt Charts. These applications also have many other features. What if someone, including yourself, decided to make a change to one of your tasks? Delete one or add one? If you created it manually, you would need to re-draw your Gantt Chart. Or suppose someone decided that there was an advantage if the logic changed or a predecessor changed? Out comes your eraser or a new blank chart to re-draw your timeline. Using software has many advantages since all you need to do is change the information on the Task Table. Using software, the Gantt Chart is dynamic, changing automatically as you enter the new information.

Some people make the decision to buy project management software to solve a problem, only to discover later that the software is merely a tool. It's not unlike purchasing a word processing application and expecting it to know what you want to write. You and your project team still need to know the basics and the relevant information to be entered into the Task Table.

In addition to drawing your Gantt Chart, the software can produce other visuals with that same data from your Task Table. The software can draw a Critical Path Method (CPM) diagram, which is similar to the Network Diagram. The software can also use the same data to show your project activities on a calendar.

Although a software application can be an excellent tool, you need to evaluate how it will best serve your needs. It could conceivably bog you down if it isn't necessary, considering the complexity of your project. Keep in mind the benefits of the software, not just the features—some of which you might never use.

If you have never seen project management software, it's a good exercise to try it out on a simple project that you may have already finished, a personal home project or the example in this chapter. Observe the pros and cons and evaluate the benefits to your project and to yourself. If the software is not available on your own computer, ask someone to give you a quick demonstration, inputting the data from your Task Table.

Use the software in its simplest forms, similar to the example in this chapter. Note that the software is capable of other functions. However, you will need to invest the time it takes to learn the application in greater detail, enter more information and update it as your project changes.

Be sure to ease into using the software gradually or you may find that it becomes an obstacle to your project instead of a help. Many people use project management applications successfully, and if your management and/or client requires it, you will need to learn it. Be proactive and become familiar with it before you are required to use it. Once you have invested time in the software training, be ready to use it while it's fresh in your mind.

Use the simplest methods to track your project based on your needs. The more complex the method, the more you pay the price in training and maintaining it. However, the benefits include greater flexibility, saving time later in your project and the availability of various analytical tools.

No matter what method you use to create your timeline, it is a valuable tool to help keep your project on schedule.

Quick Tips on Creating Your Timeline

- Create a timeline by hand for a small project
- Know where your critical path is and highlight it
- When deciding on using software, note the benefits rather than the features of the program
- Input a small project into a software program to create a timeline and observe the potential benefits to you and your projects

Chapter 8:

Keep Your Projects On Track—
Monitor Your Progress

Now that you have defined success, created your WBS, produced your Network Diagram, added the time dimension and created a timeline, you are ready to implement your project and monitor its progress.

Although establishing the timeline is part of the Planning phase, it is also used in the Monitoring phase of project management. The terms monitoring, controlling and tracking refer to the same thing and are used interchangeably.

Record Lessons Learned

As mentioned previously, keeping a project journal, diary or log is something to consider at the Monitoring phase so that you can record lessons learned from your experience. Also set up a Lessons Learned document and continually add your findings throughout the implementation of your project. Include what you learned about your schedule, budget, performance specification, staffing, reviews, technology advancements, unanticipated challenges and other items you feel are significant. In addition to documenting the problems, note how you resolved them. These lessons will be particularly helpful at the end of your project and will save you time as you and your project members evaluate what went well and what needs improvement on future projects.

Frequently people will note the mistakes to avoid on a future project but omit what worked well for them. Always include the things that worked well so you can replicate them. Do not rely on luck.

As you monitor your progress, record how much time and money it took for each task, activity and work package. Then compare them to your estimates. This actual versus planned feedback will help you improve future estimates. When you use a Tracking Gantt Chart, your visual will show two lines for each activity—the actual and planned.

Remember the Three Most Important Things to Track

It all boils down to Time, Cost and Performance. Keep track of all three and your project will be successful.

Are you doing what you said you would do, when you were supposed to do it? Since you already identified your tasks, how they fit together and when they need to take place, all you have left to do is keep a pulse on your timeline and do everything it takes to make it happen.

Keep track of the critical path. Any delay will delay your project. Also be aware of any delays on your other paths, especially those that have little slack time, or you may realize that suddenly you have a new critical path.

Watch Out for Showstoppers

In Chapter 4, we identified what could cause your project to be late, run over budget or not be to specification. Obstacles, or showstoppers, are major occurrences that can emerge at any time, throwing a monkey wrench into the progress of a project.

Consider these four questions to help you deal with showstoppers:

1. How will you know when they happen?
2. What corrective actions will you take?
3. How will it take place?
4. Who will do it?

You may have dodged some bullets, allowing your project to be ahead of schedule, but other obstacles may be lurking. Successful project managers keep a watchful eye out for showstoppers—those high-risk activities that could prevent your project from having a successful outcome. In the Monitoring phase, continue to be aware of potential obstacles and how your project is going to stay on track.

When an activity is critical, check on its status well before the deadline is imminent. As the deadline approaches, it may be too late to rectify the situation. If any activity involves a potential showstopper, track it closely. If you are dependent on others, inquire about how things are progressing and ensure they know when you expect the task to be completed. Successful project managers can also remove obstacles on critical activities by inquiring about what they can do to smooth the way. They are also available and approachable, keeping a pulse on the project without micromanaging.

Although most showstoppers will affect your critical path, it is advisable to be aware of additional concurrent activities on other paths that may slip under the radar. Track long-delivery items. Even though other people may be responsible for an activity, make sure they are on track. You can be held responsible for what someone else does. Know your options and alternate solutions that will keep the project on time, to spec and within budget.

Monitor Your Progress

The method you use to keep track of your project depends on the length of your project, its complexity and how critical it is. Avoid excessive monitoring. Plan ahead. In the Planning phase, identify the type and number of reviews that are needed for your project:

- **Minor projects** normally entail a casual type of review where the project manager is available and approachable as needed, commonly known as the observation method, personal inspection or managing by wandering around (MWA). Minor reviews, which are generally not in writing, help you build rapport and the sense of camaraderie with the people you are depending on for the success of your project. Once you establish rapport and mutual trust, people are more willing to tell you what you need to know about the project. Observation and managing by wandering around are also used on major and important projects, together with more formal methods of review.

- **Typical projects** utilize regular meetings and written progress or status reports to monitor their progress. Depending on the length of your project, these meetings and reports may take place weekly, monthly or even daily. Progress or status reports are helpful when they indicate which activities have been started and finished or to what extent they are complete. Typical projects also complement regular meetings and reports with a casual approach of observation and managing by wandering around. One drawback is requiring too many reports and repeated meetings, wasting valuable time.

- **Major projects** that are critical and complex may require a more sophisticated approach. These projects are often reviewed or audited by someone outside of your project, department or organization. The reviewers may include clients, customers, upper management and/or review boards. Anyone who needs to approve or sign off on your project falls into this category. The more important your review, the more preparation will be needed to anticipate questions that may be asked. For major reviews, consider presenting a dry run to your project team to confirm your readiness. Since reviews for major projects may require substantial time, include them in your Network Diagram and timeline or you may find yourself off-schedule.

For large projects it is impractical to review everything; instead, focus on major issues and, of course, critical path activities.

Select one of your current or upcoming projects. In the space below, write down all the things you need to do to monitor your project:

_____

_____

_____

_____

Next, take action and commit to doing them.

From time to time, projects will unavoidably go off-target; if they didn't, the need for someone to manage them would cease to exist. Your job is to monitor your projects and notice when something is starting to go astray, and then take immediate corrective action to get it back on track before it prolongs your project or makes it go over budget or off-spec. Lost time may be recovered during the later stages of your project. Being aware of slack time and available resources will help you get your project back on track.

Take Control of Meetings

Since meetings are typically the most time-consuming method of review, they have the greatest potential of being helpful. Yet meetings also hold the greatest likelihood of taking up too much time. To prevent this predicament, take control of your meetings. Assert yourself even when you are not in charge of the meeting. Make suggestions to improve the effectiveness of your meetings. Some of the most common suggestions are listed below:

- Have an agenda
- Start on time
- Have appropriate people in attendance
- Document results and action items

Establish Ground Rules for Your Meetings

The most important thing you can do to enhance your meetings is to address this question directly: "What must you and your project team members do to improve your meetings?" In fact, an agenda item at the end of each meeting could be this simple question: "What can we do to improve our next meeting?"

Another suggestion is to begin by establishing ground rules, using the input of everyone. Request one of your team members to record the suggestions on a flip chart while you or someone else facilitates the feedback. This will take only a few minutes, but this activity has the potential of saving a lot of time. The most powerful part of establishing ground rules is that the group decides how they want their meeting to function. Because they feel empowered, they will be more inclined to follow the consensus of the group. It will not be necessary to establish ground rules in future meetings unless they are to be used as a reminder or to make a revision. Check to see that your ground rules are SMART—Specific, Measurable, Agreed-upon, Realistic and Time-framed. Whatever is not working at your meetings can be corrected using ground rules.

Consider your meetings as mini-projects, with a beginning, an end and a path for completion. Practice good project management skills during the meeting.

What ground rules do you want to see in your meetings? List them below:

_____

_____

_____

_____

Select a meeting that you expect to attend in the near future and facilitate the ground rules that the group generates and agrees to. List these ground rules below:

_____

_____

_____

_____

Add Creativity, Fun and Humor to Your Meetings

When people are not participating in your meetings and you want them to share information, break them up into small groups. Facilitate an exercise that requires them to discuss whatever topic you want them to brainstorm. Have the group pick a spokesperson. Once the designated time limit is up, ask each spokesperson to share one item their group generated. Call on each group in a similar fashion and keep going until all groups have exhausted their findings. In all probability, additional ideas surfaced during this creative exercise.

Since so many people dread going to meetings, give your gathering a different label. Be innovative. Whether you decide to call them celebrations, jamborees or anything with a positive connotation, imagine people eagerly anticipating them, arriving on time and greeting one another in an upbeat, professional manner.

Most meetings call for people to speak while they are seated. For a change of pace, ask people to stand while they speak. During short meetings, try eliminating the need for chairs. The stand-up approach gives you the freedom to conduct meetings anywhere, even outdoors or in an environment away from the usual workplace. The creative approach to meetings enlivens your project, but be forewarned, creativity may be contagious.

Use nameplates to identify participants. Even if only one person doesn't know or remember another person's name, a simple nameplate is an asset. Have each participant fold a plain piece of paper into thirds and print their first name with a bold marking pen. This will encourage everyone to interact on a first-name basis.

Consider planning something fun for longer meetings. One brief exercise might be to ask your participants to select a creative adjective name pertaining to them that begins with the first letter of their first name (e.g., Productive Pat, Thorough Tom). Then have them place their adjective name on their nameplate above their first name. To tailor this exercise to your specific group, ask "What word describes a behavioral trait of a positive project manager that begins with the first letter of your first name?"

What creative and entertaining ideas would you like to see in your meetings? List them below:

_____

_____

_____

_____

Select a meeting that you will attend in the near future. Facilitate with your attendees what creative and entertaining ideas they would welcome. List them below:

_____

_____

_____

_____

Quick Tips on Monitoring Your Project

- Keep a file on lessons learned

- Know where your critical path is, so your project will stay on schedule

- Commit to monitoring your project

- Know what reviews are needed and build in appropriate time

- At the end of your day, plan the next day. Prioritize. What are the most important things that will make the most difference? Ask others this question.

- Stay focused and avoid interruptions that deter you from reaching your target, but stay alert and open to breakthrough ideas

- Establish meeting ground rules

- Make your meetings creative and fun to attend

- Start your meetings with each person relating something positive that occurred since the last meeting

- End your meetings with each person expressing appreciation or acknowledging something constructive

- Practice organization and etiquette skills during meetings within your community

MEETINGS
The Practical Alternative to Work.

Chapter 9:

Communicate With Confidence

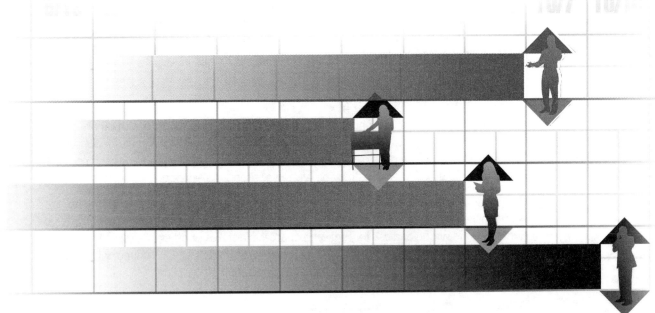

Effective communication is vital to the success of your project regardless of which stage you are in. Defining success, creating your WBS, producing your Network Diagram, adding the time dimension and creating a timeline all require communication, whether written or oral. No matter what your position, you can still be a role model by demonstrating exceptional project management skills.

When communicating with others on projects, consider these three essential concepts:

- Communicate in terms of Time, Cost and Performance
- Use the SMART acronym for clarity
- Keep the lines of communication open and value everyone's perspective

At least once a month, communicate by using brief, written progress reports for each project, whether or not they are required. This will keep you straight and remind others to focus on the goals of the projects.

Build Rapport and Trust

Much of what we learned in kindergarten can also be applied to working with others on projects, as well as in life—that is, maintain a courteous and professional attitude. Successful project teams develop a code of behavior, thereby establishing attitudes, values and core principles to follow. These codes may be written or simply understood.

There are myriad ways to build exceptional rapport with your project team; for example: smile, make eye contact, listen, shake hands, understand other people's needs, acknowledge when you are wrong and ask for forgiveness, accept mistakes of others, use specific names when addressing people and offer to jump in and help. The better you connect with people, the more inclined they will be to trust you and cooperate.

Take the Positive Approach

Avoid using the words "not" and "no." Tell people what you *can do*, instead of what you can't do for them. "Here's what I *can do*" is an example of a constructive phrase. Always look for win-win solutions. Gather as much information as you can about what the other person needs. Let people know you care about what they want, while you remain respectfully assertive and truthful.

Be upfront. If you make a promise just to get someone off your back, it will come back to haunt you later. Be realistic. Communicate with integrity and do what you say. The customer service slogan "Underpromise, Overdeliver" also applies when communicating with others on projects. Treat everyone as if they were a customer and success will be yours.

Speak with confidence and enthusiasm. When speaking or writing about your project, avoid using conditional terms such as hope, might, perhaps, possibly, if and maybe. Would you have much confidence in someone if they used the following words?

- We *hope* to get this project done on time

- This new plan *might* work

Watch your "but." Steer clear of using the word "but" as much as possible, because it tends to negate what precedes it. Instead, replace "but" with "and," or, better yet, remove the "but" whenever possible. The following are examples of what not to use.

- I'd like to do what you said, but …

- Your project looks good, but. …

When you communicate, be as positive as you can and be honest.

Ask Open-ended Questions

When you ask someone "Do you have any problems on this project?," it's too easy for them to respond with "Yes" or "No." The person answering this question may be thinking, "I'd better not tell the project manager or she'll think I'm inept." The person might also be thinking, "He isn't treating me fairly, so I'll let him discover the problems himself." You never know what's going on in someone else's head, so be a wise professional and treat everyone with respect and courtesy.

Ask questions that stimulate discussion. For example, "What problems could surface to delay this project?" Phrasing the question in this manner stimulates thought and dialogue. It also affords you the opportunity to collect more information than you would have acquired with a simple "Yes" or "No" answer.

Use "I" Statements

Abrasive statements like "You're always late with the information I need" or "Why are you always over budget?" inhibit communication.

An effective approach is to state specific facts and expectations rather than attacking the person. Use a straightforward request such as "In order to present our budget to management by the end of the week, I need your estimates for this project by noon tomorrow."

Avoid using "always" and "never." Besides, these words are seldom true so simply stick to the facts.

"I" statements help to convey respect. Use "I" statements especially when tensions run high or you are about to lose your cool. Comments like "You're always missing your deadlines" only create defensiveness.

Instead, communicate your feelings with respect. "I feel frustrated when we miss a deadline." "I appreciate your full cooperation and assistance in meeting our deadlines." This type of dialogue gives you the ability to articulate situations, behaviors and feelings rather than being aggressive and attacking the person. "I" statements also acknowledge ownership of the problem (i.e., "It's not just my problem or your problem, it's our problem.").

Use the SMART Approach

The main reason why people don't do what you want them to is simply this—they are not exactly sure what you expect them to do. They may think they know what you want, but that doesn't guarantee the outcome will correspond with your expectations.

Like the railroad project that begins simultaneously at opposite ends, when they finally come together the tracks don't quite match up at the planned intersection. Unlike the railroad fiasco, effective communication is SMART—Specific, Measurable, Agreed-upon, Realistic and Time-framed.

State the facts. "I need the draft drawings for the prototype by 4:00 p.m. this Thursday." Once you state your needs, ask for agreement, "Can we agree on that?" You will either get an agreement or you will have an opportunity to negotiate. This will either make the goal more realistic for the person doing the work or it will trigger a discussion about how to make this requirement feasible.

Handling Criticism, Complaints and Blame

No matter how good your intentions, someone is destined to criticize you. Negativity seems to be a common human trait, perhaps because of repeated exposure to, and conditioning from, watching television, reading the news or surfing the Web. Negativity, criticism and gossip help to sell copy and heighten curiosity. Sitcoms, commercials on television and Web sites on the Internet regularly lampoon and criticize people. It may be amusing to watch, but when it happens to you in real life, it lowers your self-confidence and self-esteem.

We all make mistakes. That's life. As long as your intentions are good, view your mistakes as learning experiences. Taking calculated risks is a positive leadership trait. Provided your calculated risk doesn't jeopardize your project, business, community or society and it is legal and ethical, empower yourself to take risks that allow you to grow and find better ways of doing things. Be on the alert for breakthrough ideas. Sometimes you need to ask for forgiveness instead of permission. Empower yourself.

Complaining is a negative activity unless you are communicating with someone who has the authority, ability and willingness to change the situation. When someone comes to you with a grievance, turn the conversation around and reframe it so it becomes more optimistic. Instead of telling a person what they should do, ask questions like these:

- What can you do to make this situation better?

- Is this really true? Why do you think that?

- What good things are happening on this project?

Help people see the positive in situations. Problems and obstacles will inevitably occur on most projects. Instead of focusing on the stack of stumbling blocks, reframe them—look at them as stepping stones to success. After all, overcoming a challenge can be an exhilarating learning experience. Prevent the contagion of negativity from becoming an epidemic. When you redirect your energy and focus on the tremendous progress that has been made thus far, you may have an outbreak of positive energy on your hands.

Know the Other Person's Preferred Method of Communication

Do you know people who don't answer their voice mail or e-mail messages? Has anyone ever brushed you off when you walked into their office because they were too busy or preoccupied with other things?

The best method of communicating with people is to select whatever works best for them. Let them take the lead. No matter how you receive it, your objective is to get the information you need for the project. When in doubt, determine the preferred method of communicating with each person you deal with. In some cases, a person may have more than one preferred method of communicating with you, depending on the type of information you need. All you have to do is ask them.

Some people are hesitant to share information in a group; for them, one-to-one communication may work best. Communication is not one-size-fits-all. Adapt to each person's style of communication. Appreciate the differences that make each of us unique.

Know the Needs of the Other Person

In addition to using the appropriate method of communicating with people, be sure to take into account their specific needs as well. If you provide too much detail to someone in upper-management, he or she may not pay attention to what is really important. Likewise, if you are not detailed enough when you communicate with your peers, they may not receive crucial information.

Some people may simply move forward, armed only with the information at hand, without asking questions. The end result might be different from what you expect. Tailor your method of communication to the meet the specific needs of your project team members, support staff, upper-management, customers, clients, vendors and anyone else you have contact with.

Tune In to WIIFU and TEAM

Do you listen to WIIFU? These call letters stand for "What's In It For Us?" When communicating, consider what everyone's needs are and the benefits they will receive in terms of your project being completed successfully. Communicate the benefits, letting everyone know why something needs to be done, helping them see the advantages of their project organization, other team members, customers, clients and themselves.

When you include the tasks and activities from others you are depending on in your Network Diagram and Timeline, it becomes clear to everyone that their activities must be completed before other activities can proceed. The better that alignment, the more smoothly your project will flow. The "A" in the SMART acronym represents "Agreed-upon." This agreement helps everyone move toward their common goal as a TEAM—Together Everyone Achieves More.

The Lost Art of Listening

Listening is often the least-used device in the project management tool bag. Some project managers do not value listening unless it means listening to them. The problem is that without listening you may be going down a road full of potholes or perhaps a blind alley. Have you ever ignored someone's advice or directions? You may have discovered a shortcut to save time, only to find yourself on a road that is under construction in a dangerous neighborhood. Even if we listen to words of wisdom and advice, this could still happen.

If you think you have all the answers, think again. Everyone has answers. As a successful project leader you need to ask the right questions, listen to the feedback and then make a decision.

Successful project managers listen attentively in order to better understand the perspectives of others. Leaders do not need to know all the answers, but they do need to ask the right questions. They ask for help, network, call a Life-Line, synergize and build new relationships with people who possess the expertise they want. They depend on others who have the expertise and skills needed for the successful outcomes of their projects.

Listen to Your Own Voice Mail Greeting

Have you ever listened to the message on someone's voice mail greeting and wondered, "What were they thinking?" Listen to your own voice mail greeting and ask others to give you their honest opinion relating to the following:

- How confident does your message sound?
- How upbeat and positive is your greeting?
- Is it too abrupt?
- Is your message conversational or does it sound like you're reading it?
- Will the person know who you are and where you're from?
- Are you talking too rapidly?
- Are you talking down to the caller, as if they were a fifth grader?
- Is your message too long?

If your greeting must be lengthy and there is an available option to avoid listening to it in its entirety, mention this fact early on.

Save your motivational quotations and charming limericks for another venue. A short, direct, friendly message works best. If you insist on adding humor, use it sparingly and make it tasteful and appropriate.

Leave Clear Voice Messages for Others

Many of the above considerations also apply to leaving voice mail messages for someone else. Below are some additional suggestions.

Don't rehash the same information. When you realize this is a habit of yours, prepare ahead and jot down notes so that the message you leave is succinct and well-organized.

Avoid messages requesting the other person to call you back. Although this may be appropriate at times, at least let the other person know what you want, when you want it, when you are available if they need to talk with you and the best way for them to get that information to you. This may allow you to get your answer without ever directly talking to the person and saves time for both parties, and if deemed necessary, it provides a window of opportunity for live telephone access.

If you are upset, allow yourself time to "cool off" before responding too hastily, saving you needless embarrassment later on.

Nonverbals Speak Volumes

Our actions speak louder than words so use them to your advantage. People listen not only to what you say, but to how you say it. Speak with confidence and enthusiasm.

Maintain a personal appearance that demonstrates confidence and professionalism. People will treat you differently when you dress neatly, keep yourself groomed, have proper hygiene and behave in a manner congruent with what you say.

For your amusement, conduct your own experiment outside of the workplace. Contrast the diverse reactions you get when you dress casually versus when you dress for success.

Handle Conflicts Effectively

If deadlines slip, budgets are exceeded or other challenges develop on your project, conflicts result. Communication is interesting because it is used to resolve conflicts, yet at times, it can be the root of conflict, which is stressful. Some quick and easy tips to help resolve conflicts are:

- Stay calm
- Use the person's name
- Shake hands
- Decide to work together and resolve the conflict
- Visualize success in dealing with a difficult individual or situation
- Seek a win-win solution
- Stick to the facts and current issues, avoiding personality conflicts and digging up ancient history
- Focus on active listening, avoiding other distractions
- Paraphrase to be sure you each understand the other's point of view
- Hold off formulating a response to win; instead seek a win-win solution

Seek Win-Win Solutions

When resolving conflicts, consider the following:

- How important is the goal?
- How important is the relationship?
- Are you dependent on the person for the success of your project?
- How much are you willing to give in order to accommodate the other person?

The answers to these questions will help you decide which method you will use to resolve conflicts in any given situation.

Conflict Handling Modes

Following is a summary of the various types of Conflict Handling Modes. Note that most have more than one name, as people use a variety of terms to denote the same thing.

Withdrawal / Avoidance: This method works on the unimportant. Don't sweat the small stuff.

- Neither party satisfies their concerns or needs
- Neither side talks or listens
- Low assertiveness or cooperation by both parties
- Low importance of needs and goals by both parties
- Low importance of relationship by both parties
- Lose-Lose situation: Neither party wins

Smoothing / Accommodation / Giving In: This method can be viewed by your team members as a sign of weakness, especially when they are seen as giving in all the time. Some resentment can develop when used too often.

- One party's needs are satisfied at the expense of the other party
- Low assertiveness by party giving in
- High cooperation by party giving in
- Low importance of the needs and goals of party giving in
- High importance of relationship by party giving in
- Lose-Win: One party wins and one loses

Compromising / Bargaining: This method can lead to resentment and bitterness if either person leaves with the feeling that what they lost was something they needed.

- Both parties give up some of their concerns to satisfy the other party
- Some assertiveness and cooperation by both parties
- Some importance of needs and goals by both parties
- Some importance of relationship by both parties
- Partial loss and partial win for both parties

Forcing / Competing / Demanding: This is the "My way or the highway" approach. There are times when this method works, such as with a safety issue, a crisis or when dealing with something that is illegal or immoral and when there is no time or need to call a meeting. The ship is sinking, someone needs to make a decision, and it has to be made right now. If this method is used routinely, people will not cooperate. Eventually it leads to a Lose-Lose situation.

- One party satisfies their concerns at the other party's expense
- High assertiveness becomes aggression by one party
- Low cooperation on part of the aggressor
- High importance of needs and goals
- Low importance of relationship
- Win-Lose

Confrontation / Collaboration / Cooperation / Problem Solving: This win-win method is the most successful in dealing with issues on projects. It may take more time to resolve the conflict in this way, but ultimately it is more satisfying and empowering. Both parties understand that conflicts are a normal part of their projects and they have the confidence to resolve them respectfully.

- Both parties discover new and creative ways to satisfy both of their concerns through active listening

- High assertiveness and cooperation on part of both parties

- High importance of needs and goals by both sides

- High importance of relationship on both sides

- Win-Win

Depending on your circumstances, you might use any of these methods from time to time, but seeking a win-win solution is the most successful method used in project management. It is gratifying to overcome a stressful relationship or situation. Being aware of what causes the conflicts is the first step in managing them.

What issues are creating conflicts in your workplace and your projects? List them on the left side of the section below. On the right side, brainstorm ways that you and your project team can effectively minimize each conflict. Then take appropriate action.

Conflict issues: Conflict minimizers:

_____   _____

_____   _____

_____   _____

_____   _____

_____   _____

_____   _____

Sharpen Your Communication Skills

Generally, the more technical-minded the individuals, the less likely they are to value the benefits of effective communication. In addition to continuing your education in the technical and computer arenas, it is advantageous to include training on the softer side of projects. Take at least one seminar or workshop every year in a non-technical area, which could include:

- Clear writing, business writing, technical writing, grammar and punctuation
- Presentation skills, speaking effectively, overcoming the fear of public speaking
- Listening
- People skills, working with difficult people
- Overcoming conflict
- Communicating effectively

Even though a seminar, workshop or conference may not at first appear to be of particular interest to you, allow yourself to attend. You may discover a new way of looking at things when you least expect it. You may also acquire a creative edge you can apply to your projects or other fields of interest.

Avail yourself of everyday opportunities to practice first-rate writing skills, including e-mails, and make a habit of using proper grammar, correct spelling and punctuation in all written communications.

Seize every opportunity to speak before a group. Incorporating your newfound communication skills into your everyday work will become second nature. The more practice you afford yourself, the more confident and eloquent you will become. With little additional effort, you can focus on making sure that you:

- Have organization, flow and purpose in what you're communicating
- Use normal conversational language
- Provide appropriate eye contact
- Use natural gestures and body language

Connect with groups that offer you the opportunity to practice presentation skills and offer constructive feedback for improvement. Such groups include community, civic and service groups. In addition to helping you polish your public speaking capabilities, these groups will assist you in building self-confidence and sharpening your organizational, listening and leadership skills.

Improving your communication skills should be an ongoing endeavor appropriate for all aspects of your professional and personal life, regardless of where your projects are. You may need to apply these skills sooner than you think, so don't put it off.

In the space below, list the communication skills that you and your project team need to improve:

_____

_____

_____

_____

Quick Tips on Communicating With Confidence

- Communicate in terms of Time, Cost and Performance
- Use the SMART acronym when communicating
- Be a role model of exceptional communication techniques
- Build rapport with everyone
- Tell people what you can do, instead of what you can't do
- Build trust and empowerment in your project team
- Ask open-ended questions
- Learn how other people prefer to communicate
- Understand the needs of others
- Listen attentively to understand
- Display confidence in your communication
- Manage conflicts, seek win-win solutions
- Practice speaking in front of a group at every opportunity

Chapter 10:

Stimulate the Spirit in Your Project

> *"If you did all the things in life that you were truly capable of, you would literally astound yourself."*
>
> — *Thomas Edison*

A positive, stimulating and professional environment brings out the best in your team, regardless of what stage of the project they are currently working on. The more everyone looks forward to coming to the workplace with a positive attitude, eagerly anticipating the venture, the more productive and joyful the experience will be. An "I can't wait to see what exciting things will happen" attitude will unite your team so that together they can solve any problems that come their way.

Most managers agree they can train nearly all people to perform the technical side of any job, but motivating them is a challenge since it must come from within. Although most people are motivated, there is no guarantee that they will be motivated to do the work required of them. On the other hand, it is possible to plant the seeds of inspiration by creating a favorable environment that will foster growth.

Managers who hire or acquire project members based solely on technical expertise are sometimes troubled by an individual's inability to get along with the other team members. When possible, consider the attitude, motivation, dependability and people skills of those you are considering adding to your project team. What you see is what you get. However, you can bring out the best in everyone by creating a friendly, creative, nurturing and positive environment.

Recognize what motivates people. Start with yourself. What motivates you? Take a few minutes and write your answers below:

_____

_____

_____

_____

Next ask each member of your project to make a list of at least ten things that motivate them. The only way to ascertain what motivates others is to ask them.

People are never too busy to do the things they are truly passionate about.

Do the Things You Like

When people on your project are performing specific activities that they like to do, are good at or want to become better at, they presumably are inspired and motivated by the experience. Start again with yourself.

On your project:

What activities do you like to do?

_____

_____

_____

_____

What activities do you prefer not to do?

_____

_____

_____

_____

What activities are you very good at?

_____

_____

_____

_____

What activities would you like to become better at?

_____

_____

_____

_____

Although it's not always possible to do what you like to do or what you want to become better at, the more you engage in these activities the more you will grow to enjoy your experience. You may also find your personal goals to be more in alignment with your project goals. When you enjoy your work, it is no longer just work; it becomes work with a meaningful purpose.

Every person is wired differently. Each has a unique combination of likes and dislikes, so you can't assume that you know what a person likes, dislikes or wants to improve on unless you ask them. When you assemble a new team, have them take part in an exercise. Ask each person to take a few minutes and answer the same four questions that appear on the previous page.

Catch People Doing Things Right

Too often, people are quick to point out the mistakes of others and ignore what they are doing right. Most people appreciate a sincere compliment where it is due. Positive feedback motivates them to carry out similar activities so they can repeat the response. When an individual knows that you like and appreciate what they do, you will probably see a repeat performance.

Successful project managers see problems and mistakes as opportunities for growth. Instead of calling attention to someone's mistake, they ask, "What can you do to avoid this in the future?" or "What did you learn from this?"

One factor in creating a more positive working environment is to focus on people's strengths instead of their weaknesses. In their book *The One Minute Manager*, Ken Blanchard and Spencer Johnson point out the value of catching people doing something right and telling them about it.

Challenge yourself and your colleagues to catch 10 people doing something right on a given day. Make a list on the following page, noting who did it, what they did and their reactions. In addition, refer to the Appendix D on page 142 and copy the sheet to make people aware of the importance of catching people doing things right. Be sure to include support staff, clients, management and yourself.

1. _____

2. _____

3. _____

4. _____

5. _____

6. _____

7. _____

8. _____

9. _____

10. _____

Focus on Strengths

As you and your project team members focus on catching people doing things right, you will notice many strengths in everyone, including yourself. During interviews or performance evaluations, you have undoubtedly been asked to point out your strengths.

Although some people are reluctant to mention their strong points out of fear they will be perceived as bragging or being conceited, others who possess a high level of self-esteem are keenly aware of their strengths and are highly effective at maximizing them.

What are your strengths? List as many as you can:

_____

_____

_____

_____

As you recognize additional strengths that you did not include above, add them to your list. This is a dynamic process, so naturally you will want to keep an ongoing tally of your strengths in a word processing document or a hard folder for quick reference.

What strengths do your project team members see in one another? Sometimes we don't realize the strengths other people see in us. Help team members become aware of each other's strengths.

For an interesting exercise, ask each person on your project team to take a blank 8½ x 11-inch piece of paper and have them write or print their first name at the top with a bold marking pen.

Then, similar to the activity suggested in Chapter 8, in the meetings section, have your team members select a creative, positive adjective-name and write it alongside their name on the top of the page (for example: Loyal Linda, Systematic Scott, Motivating Mary). Have each person post their paper on a wall or table so that others can write something positive about each person. To enhance the element of fun, encourage them to use a variety of colors and creative symbols. This exercise allows people to see the strengths that other people see in them.

What creative ideas would your project team like to do to bring additional fun and inspiration to your workplace? Ask each person to share their ideas and tabulate them below. Decide which you can implement, then take appropriate action:

_____

_____

_____

_____

Keep a "Happy" File

Whenever someone sends you a complimentary e-mail or letter or pays you a compliment about your work, note it. Cut and paste or enter it into a word processing document. File these letters or memos in a folder. Some people refer to this as a "Happy File," others call it a "Warm and Fuzzy" file. Give it whatever name you like. Every so often, you will come across this file. Even if you don't take the time to read it again, simply noticing it will trigger you to remember the positive things people have observed about you.

Work Hard, Play Hard

Have fun on your project in the process of producing quality deliverables on time and within budget. Bring into play your team's creativity and enjoy the endeavor. Don't worry if other people think you are wacky. As long as it works for your team and doesn't interfere with others, go for it.

Many successful project teams have fun together outside, as well as inside, the workplace. Getting to know your project team members outside the official work setting has the potential to bring a team closer together. Attend seminars, conferences and retreats together. Share information, ideas and experiences that will unite your team.

Hold Lunch and Learn meetings with team members, taking turns presenting various topics of interest. Not only will everyone learn something, but your team also will be rotating the task of making presentations before a group—an opportunity that is avoided by many but a fundamental leadership skill to develop and refine. Reading, listening to and watching the same motivational and educational materials with a follow-up discussion helps put the team on the same page.

Successful project managers might do some of the following:

- Give their project a creative and humorous name

- Create team names for each group on their project

- Make a picture calendar of team members

- Create a special bulletin board

- Welcome new team members

- Interview each team member with name, photo and interests

- Make a project scrapbook

- Take photos of the team at the project kick-off and capture action shots at various stages of the project, including its successful completion

Brainstorm the following question with your team: How can we create more fun and excitement in our project environment? List the results below:

_____

_____

_____

_____

Focus on the Positive—When Things Seem Hopeless

Every project will have its ups and downs, as will everyone on the project team. The positive aspect of being part of a team is that when one person is down, others are around to lend an ear and a helping hand to lift their spirits.

When things seem hopeless, instead of digging the hole of despair even deeper by complaining about how bad things are, encourage others to see the brighter side of the situation.

To help turn the tide from pessimism to optimism, brainstorm the following questions with your team:

- What is good about your project?
- What is good about this organization?
- What can we do to make things better?
- On a scale of 1 to 10, where are we now? What will it take to make this experience a 10 (the highest)?

Feeling overworked, stressed out and unappreciated defeats motivation. Sometimes it may seem like the only reward for getting a project done well is being assigned more projects. If this happens to you, empower yourself to discuss the workload with your manager to make it realistic rather than unattainable. Be enthusiastic. Practice positive self-talk. Have an "I can do it" mindset, not an "I can do anything" attitude. Reach for the stars but stay grounded with a sense of reality.

Cancel-Cancel Negative Talk

When you hear negative self-talk or when someone says something negative to you, refuse to believe it. In such cases, Jack Canfield (CEO of Chicken Soup for the Soul Enterprises, Inc.) suggests saying to yourself "Cancel-cancel" or adding the phrase "up until now."

For example, if your inner voice says, "We never get our projects done on time," end the phrase with "up until now," or say to yourself: "Cancel-cancel."

Say "no" to falling into the trap of negativity. Remain positive to the extent that you can, and when you feel yourself slipping, take action to pull yourself up again. Ask a friend or co-worker to join forces with you. Support each other. Read and listen to motivational resources.

Maintain the Flow of Creative Ideas

Be receptive to new and creative ideas. You never know when a breakthrough idea will surface or a competitive edge will be realized. Avoid productivity-killing phrases that shut ideas down. Remarks like "That will never work" or "We tried that before" could prevent a person from sharing more ideas or stifle others from offering their thoughts.

No matter how great you think an idea is, there typically will be someone who thinks it isn't so great. In fact, later on you might even agree with them. Even so, it is imperative to keep your creative juices flowing. The odds are that at least one in ten of your ideas will be a good one. Remember, you have endless capabilities for creative ideas as long as you keep them flowing.

On a piece of paper, jot down ideas as they come to you, even if it means tossing them in the trash afterward. Some of your best ideas may come to you as you are falling asleep or waking up. Have a pencil and pad within reach so you can capture your ideas on paper immediately.

When you find yourself daydreaming, think of it as a form of meditation and jot down your ideas on paper as they pop up. The normal ebb and flow of our attention span tends to accelerate when we are sedentary too long. Although focusing on the matter at hand is often the desired goal, daydreaming is inevitable. Accept your creative instincts and go with the flow.

Take calculated risks. Making mistakes is only human. Bear in mind, errors are an integral part of the creative process. What would you and/or your team members like to do, but for some reason are holding back on? List each one on the left side below. On the right side, note what you can do to implement each one.

Want to: **How to:**

_____   _____

_____   _____

_____   _____

_____   _____

_____   _____

What does your project team currently do to create a motivating environment?

_____

_____

_____

How can you add more positive energy and motivation to your workplace?

_____

_____

_____

Quick Tips to Stimulate Spirit in Your Project

- Empower yourself and ask to work on a particular project or specific task
- Catch people doing things right
- Be available and approachable
- Respect everyone
- Be a good listener
- Help create a positive environment
- Use appropriate humor in the workplace
- Discard put-downs
- Show integrity. Underpromise, overdeliver. Do what you say you will.
- Handle the instinct to micromanage, and trust others. Agree on appropriate involvement, sharing of information and progress updates.
- Encourage others to assert themselves to use and develop their skills and talents

"Surround yourself with positive people, read uplifting books and listen to audio programs that flood your mind with positive, life-affirming messages."

— *Jack Canfield*

Chapter 11:

Finish the Project—Deliver the Goods

It's nearly showtime. Now that you are almost ready to successfully present the deliverable that you agreed to at the beginning of your project, there is some light housekeeping to tend to. Tidying up and learning from your experience is an important component of the entire process.

You may have assorted activities as you approach the finish or the final act of your project, such as the following:

- User test
- Approval
- Sign-off
- Delivery
- Acceptance
- Final inspection

The Project Acceptance

The first phase of your project was to define success in terms of Time, Cost and Performance. This was also agreed upon by the designated client who would be signing off and accepting the results of your project as being done successfully at its conclusion.

It's time to deliver the goods in compliance with your contract. Provided you have defined, planned, implemented and controlled your project throughout its life cycle, there should be no surprises at the end. Your project will be approved and accepted as being successful.

Creatively Finishing Your Project

By definition, a project must have a finish date. Working on a never-ending project destroys motivation. Closure brings a feeling of accomplishment. Beware of the project that has no conclusion. It may, however, require some creativity to bring some projects to a close. When necessary negotiate to complete an agreed-upon goal that is realistic. Projects that have substantial follow-up may require a major milestone which acts as the project's culmination. The remaining work could be given a different name, allowing the original project to be considered as closed out.

Some projects have what are known as Punch Lists, which are tasks that still need to be done, even though the project has been turned over to its owner. In addition to punch lists, some projects may require follow-up documentation, such as procedures, manuals and as-built drawings. In advance, agree on what is considered necessary for the project to be complete and which activities will be considered follow-ups to tie up loose ends afterward. Even though the cost of the follow-up activities will probably be included in the budget, the project can still be regarded as complete and ready for a celebration.

Lessons Learned

Throughout every phase of your project you kept a journal, diary, log or file, noting what went well and what needed improvement in the future. Before your project is finished, perform a post-mortem with everyone associated with your project to review lessons learned. By the time you finish your project, some players already may have been reassigned to other projects and might not be available for input, so obtain their feedback before they're gone. Document the lessons learned throughout the project and review them at this stage.

Be sure to include what went well and what everyone did to make this happen so that you can replicate these achievements in the future. Note what is specific to this type of project or peculiar to this industry or client. File your findings where you and others will be able to locate them when the time comes to work on a similar project or a new project for the same client.

What lessons have you learned from past projects?

_____

_____

_____

_____

Final Reports and Documentation

Identify ahead of time what types of wrap-up reports will be needed and desired by your upper-management, client or others so that you can incorporate these activities into your schedule and budget. Give appropriate details and tailor each report accordingly. Always report in terms of Time, Cost and Performance.

Show Appreciation, Give Thanks and Celebrate

Sincere thank you's are always appreciated by those who are simply "doing their job." Although handwritten thank-you notes are commonly valued, tailor your expressions of gratitude to whatever works best in your situation, using your preferred style of communication.

Remember to thank your support team members who may have worked on your project on a part-time basis. Vary your style of thanking people and observe what appears to be most effective. As in the other aspects of your project, feedback helps everyone improve their future performance.

Plan a celebration at the end of your project. This too shows appreciation for a job well done and helps bring closure and recognition. Celebrations at major milestones during long projects help to revitalize and re-commit your team members. The celebrations need not be costly or time-consuming. Celebrate creatively and brainstorm with your project team for ideas.

What are you currently doing to celebrate your project completions?

_____

_____

_____

_____

_____

_____

How would you and your project team like to celebrate your project completions?

_____

_____

_____

_____

_____

_____

Quick Tips for When Your Project's Completed

- Provide continuing support and service
- Prepare a post-completion audit
- Reassign project personnel and other resources
- Conduct a project evaluation
- Prepare a wrap-up report for upper management
- Send letters of appreciation; include support groups
- Keep a project journal, diary or log
- Record issues
- Note surprises, problems and options
- Hold "lessons learned" meeting
- Brainstorm ideas for future success and create an action plan
- Formulate the wrap-up part of your project schedule and assign the tasks
- Prepare performance reports on all project staff as needed
- Do a self-evaluation—what would you do differently next time
- Say "Thank you" in person or in writing (handwritten)
- Give each project team member a certificate or memento

Chapter 12:

Take Care of Number One

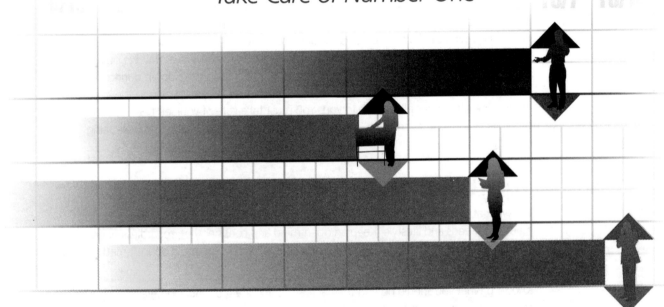

> "Life isn't about finding yourself. Life is about creating yourself."
>
> — *George Bernard Shaw*

Although you have reached the final chapter of this book, it may be the most important one. Your journey is just beginning.

Flying to a destination on an airplane is a project. It has a beginning, an end and a path for completion. It has a deliverable—arriving safely at your correct destination. It has a "Definition of Success" in terms of Time, Cost and Performance. There also are other activities dependent on each other; for instance, you can't land unless you take off. To make it fly, this project is reliant on support staff, many of whom you may never see or hear, such as mechanics and air traffic controllers. The captain and flight attendants may ask you to perform certain tasks to ensure a successful flight (project). Among these tasks is a review of the FAA safety and emergency evacuation procedures. If you have ever flown, you already know your course of action in the event that the oxygen masks drop down during flight. You would immediately place the oxygen mask on yourself before coming to the aid of others. The same principle applies to you. You must take care of yourself first. As you work on projects and journey through everyday life, remember—your health and well-being come first.

Listen to Your Body

Know what works best for you. There is more than one recipe for success, so sculpt it to meet your needs and lifestyle. Keep an open mind and consider that, regardless of how ridiculous your approach sounds to someone else, if it works for you it doesn't matter what others think.

Knowing what you should do and then actually doing it are distinctly different. Common sense isn't always common practice. When you yearn for something new or have a burning desire for more abundance in your life, write it down and visualize it happening. Getting enough sleep, practicing healthy eating habits, exercising, taking time for hobbies, making new friends and maintaining existing positive relationships are examples.

Arrive at work early and seize the quiet time of day, free of interruptions. Start working your plan. If you can't see your way clear to arrive early every day, then set a goal to be an early bird for only one day each week. To make big changes, begin with small steps. Remember the question: "How do you eat an elephant? One bite at a time." Working for only half an hour without interruption could equate to what you would usually accomplish in one or two hours of your normal work day.

Plan your work and work your plan. Determination and persistence pay off. Most people give up too soon. When you are persistent you have an advantage over the more experienced or gifted competition. Everyone is unique. Instead of comparing yourself to others, be the best "you" that you can be. There is no substitute for common sense.

Manage Stress—Nurture Your Mind, Body and Spirit

Find a quiet place, at least once a day. Be still. Take a walk, meditate, do yoga, practice tai chi, get a massage, go on a retreat, do whatever nourishes your mind, body and spirit. Practice what is within your level of comfort. Anyone can do this. There are no qualifications. All you need is an open heart and peaceful mind. Think positive thoughts about your project and everyone associated with it. Visualize everyone working together in peace and harmony. Be kind to yourself. Pat yourself on the back. Set aside some time every day to relax, maintain balance and be at peace.

Continue to sharpen your skills. Attend seminars, conferences and retreats. Read, listen to and watch motivational and educational materials. Be open and flexible to trying new things. You may discover a breakthrough idea that could change your life—when you least expect it.

Focus on the Important

Countless tasks and people vie for your time and attention every day. Are you able to do everything? Most people will admit that they can't do it all. Realizing they continually are juggling priorities, they may intend to take care of the most critical and important things first, but not always. Sometimes people get stuck in a rut and, for various reasons, wind up working on less significant tasks.

In his book *The Seven Habits of Highly Effective People*, Stephen Covey advocates "putting first things first." He recommends identifying the various hats that you wear. For example, you may be a project manager or you may have another role in your workplace. In addition, you have a host of roles associated with you personal life and your world outside of your job (e.g., roles as mother, father, sister, brother, son, daughter, officer of a professional organization, community leader or volunteer). Choose a few of these roles that are most significant to you and then, as Covey suggests, ask yourself this question: "What is the most important thing that I can do this week that would have the greatest positive impact in my role as ... ?" Keep in mind one of these roles is you. Include the things you want and need in order to nurture yourself.

Notice that Covey specifies "this week." He considers that a period of time that is not too short and not too long; in other words, a short stretch of time where you are most likely to make a more significant difference.

Ask other people the same question. Ask everyone that you depend on for the success of your projects. Phrase the question using terms you are comfortable with. For example, "On the XYZ project, what are the most important things you need to do this week?" or "What tasks will you complete this week?" Looking at the Gantt Charts for your projects will help you see what is supposed to be happening in any particular time frame. It will guide you and help you to keep your projects on track.

Action Items and Commitment

Unless you decide to apply some of the concepts addressed in this book to making some changes, your efforts will have been a complete waste of time. Your first step is to decide to make a change. But, to ensure success, always follow up with the second step—commit to taking action.

Below, make a list identifying what you need to do to make a difference in your projects in the workplace, your personal life and your community. On the left side, list what you will commit to doing. On the right side, list what actions you need to take to make each one a reality.

Commitments:

_____

_____

_____

_____

_____

Actions:

_____

_____

_____

_____

_____

A Bag of Tools
By R. L. Sharpe

Isn't it strange that princesses and kings,

And clowns that caper in sawdust rings,

And everyday people like you and me,

Are builders of eternity?

Each is given a bag of tools;

A shapeless mass, a book of rules.

And each must make, 'ere life is flown,

A stumbling block or a stepping stone.

This poem is a reminder that obstacles are an integral part of projects. Your projects need you and your project team to overcome the problems, which are like friction. Yet friction is how tools are sharpened and polished. When you look at friction as something positive, allowing you to improve in the process, your projects, along with your life, will continue to be successful.

At the end of your career of working on projects, it will be rewarding to hear people at your retirement party talking about how you excelled at completing your projects on time, within budget and of incomparable quality. But the most fulfilling of all will be to hear, "Not only were you a terrific project manager, but you were a great person, always ready to lend a hand. You helped and challenged us to be our best."

Our wish for you is that this book has made a difference in how you view your projects, as well as your life. We trust it will continue to help you take the mystery out of your projects and that it has inspired you toward continued, constant and never-ending improvement.

Quick Tips on Taking Care of Number One

- Your health and well-being come first

- Listen to your body—know what works for you

- Determination and persistence pay off

- Manage stress—nurture your mind, body and spirit

- Set aside time to relax, maintain balance and be at peace

- Continue to sharpen your skills

- Focus on the important —"What is the most important thing that I can do this week?" Ask others this question.

- Decide to change and commit to taking action

- Friction allows you to improve

- Think of life as a project—develop your own LBS (Life Breakdown Structure) in terms of Time, Cost and Performance

Glossary

Jargon, Terms and Acronyms

- **CPM:** Critical Path Method

- **Crashing the Project:** Getting the project done sooner, thereby increasing the cost

- **Critical Path:** The longest duration of a project, from start to finish

- **Dependency or Predecessor:** An activity that must be completed (or partially completed) before another specific activity can begin

- **Float or Slack Time:** The amount of time an activity can slip past its earliest completion date without delaying the rest of the project

- **Network Diagram:** A visual presentation of activities logically placed to show the flow of the project from beginning to end

- **PERT:** Program Evaluation and Review Technique

- **Scope Creep:** Changing the specification little by little, making the schedule and cost unrealistic or impossible

- **SWAG:** Scientific Wild Assumed Guess

- **WAG:** Wild Assumed Guess

- **WBS:** Work Breakdown Structure

Gantt Chart

ID#	Task Name	Duration	Predecessors	1	2	3	4	5	6	7	8	9	10	11	12	13	14	15	16	17	18	19	20
1																							
2																							
3																							
4																							
5																							
6																							
7																							
8																							
9																							
10																							
11																							
12																							
13																							
14																							
15																							
16																							
17																							
18																							
19																							
20																							
21																							
22																							
23																							
24																							
25																							
26																							
27																							
28																							
29																							
30																							

Project Management Survey

How would you rate the following areas in your organization? Circle one number for each statement.

Poor				Average					Excellent

We have a clear idea of what our projects are supposed to accomplish.
1   2   3   4   5   6   7   8   9   10

We can describe specifically the limits of our resources.
1   2   3   4   5   6   7   8   9   10

Our projects are segmented into manageable pieces.
1   2   3   4   5   6   7   8   9   10

Our projects have written schedules.
1   2   3   4   5   6   7   8   9   10

Our projects consider the perspectives of all stakeholders.
1   2   3   4   5   6   7   8   9   10

Each project team member is committed to the project's successful completion.
1   2   3   4   5   6   7   8   9   10

Our project team members build effective agreements and think win-win.
1   2   3   4   5   6   7   8   9   10

Our project team willingly follows requests of others.
1   2   3   4   5   6   7   8   9   10

Our project team is motivated to be creative and imaginative.
1   2   3   4   5   6   7   8   9   10

What prevents you from getting your projects done on-time, within budget and to specification/quality?

_____

_____

What suggestions do you have to improve your organization's project management?

_____

_____

What is working well? _____

Catch People Doing Things Right Chart

As Kenneth Blanchard and Spencer Johnson state in their book *The One-Minute Manager*, "Catch people doing something right and tell them." People usually hear only about what they are doing wrong.

Look for the good in every situation. What is good about your project and the people working on it?

Notice what people are doing right and then tell them. Include everyone you interact with. Note their name, the date and time and where and what they did right. Then tell them, at an appropriate time and place.

Name	Date	Time	What They Did Right	Where	Did I Tell Them? (Yes/No)